Writing

Aufgaben zur Textproduktion

Englisch
1.–6. Lernjahr

WRITING
Aufgaben zur Textproduktion

Im Auftrag des Verlages erarbeitet von

Dominik Eberhard, Bonn; Ulrike Flach, Köln; Anne Forder, Straßburg; Senta Friedrich, Tamm; Timo Keller, Kornthal; Martin Kohn, Frankfurt; Silke Lehmacher, Aschaffenburg; Ursula Mulla (†), München; Angela Ringel-Eichinger, Bietigheim-Bissingen; Andrea Rohoff, Hannover; Cecile Rossant, Berlin; Martina Schroeder, Stedtlingen; Jana Schubert, Genf; Bärbel Schweitzer M.A., Staufen; Jennifer Seidl, München

In Zusammenarbeit mit der Englischredaktion

Christiane Kallenbach (Projektleitung), Doreen Arnold

Titelbild

Yvonne Thron, Berlin (Stift, Körper (M)); iStockphoto, Calgary (Jungenkopf: simmosimosa (M))

Umschlaggestaltung

Yvonne Thron (designcollective), Berlin

Layout und technische Umsetzung

graphitecture book & edition

www.cornelsen.de

1. Auflage, 1. Druck 2014

© 2014 Cornelsen Schulverlag GmbH, Berlin

Druck: Stürtz GmbH, Würzburg

ISBN 978-3-06-033366-0

PEFC zertifiziert
Dieses Produkt stammt aus nachhaltig
bewirtschafteten Wäldern und kontrollierten
Quellen.
www.pefc.de
PEFC/04-31-1404

Liebe Lehrerin, lieber Lehrer,

wir haben für Sie eine Materialsammlung zusammengestellt, die Aufgaben zur Textproduktion für die Jahrgangsstufen 5 bis 10 bereitstellt. Diese lassen sich sowohl im Übungs- wie im Testkontext einsetzen. Alle Aufgabenblätter stehen Ihnen als Kopiervorlagen zur Verfügung.

Wir wünschen Ihnen und Ihren Schülerinnen und Schülern viel Erfolg.

Ihre Englischredaktion

Who am I?

Write about you. The mind map can help you.

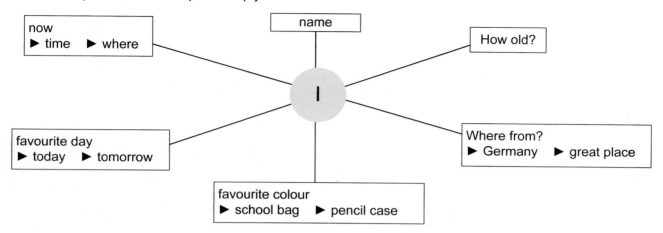

now
▶ time ▶ where

name

How old?

favourite day
▶ today ▶ tomorrow

I

Where from?
▶ Germany ▶ great place

favourite colour
▶ school bag ▶ pencil case

You can start like this:

Hi, My Name ...

The things in my school bag

Complete the mind map with three things that you have in your school bag and four things that you have in your pencil case.

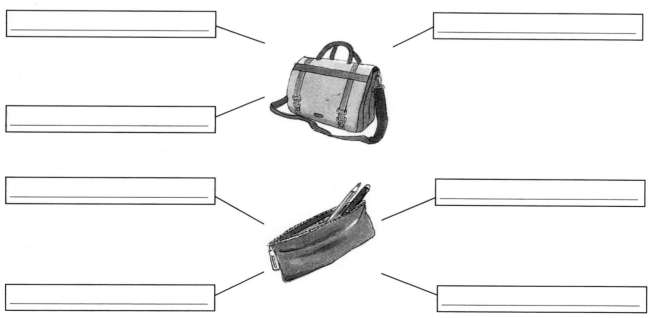

Write what you have in your school bag.

You can start like this:

In my school bag I've got ...

Illustrationen: **Constanze Schargan**, Berlin

A morning in my family

Complete the mind map. The ideas in the box can help you.

Write what you do and what you don't do. Write what your mum does and what she doesn't do.

Write what your dad does and what he doesn't do. Have you got a brother or a sister?

Write what they do and what they don't do.

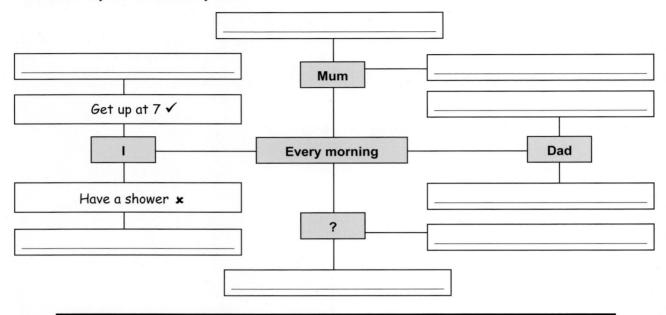

Ideas:
get up – clean my teeth – have a shower – get dressed – make my bed – get things ready –
make breakfast – have breakfast – read newspaper – feed pets – go to school – go to work

My family

Write a short text about your family. Here are some ideas.

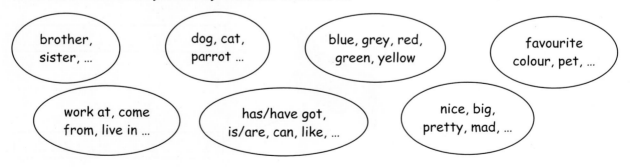

You can start like this:

I've got a sister …
She is … years old.
My …

The Life of Brian Moody

Look at the mind map and write about Brian. What does he have to do at home or at school?
What can he do at home or at school? What does he often, sometimes or never do with his friends?
You can also write what Brian doesn't have to do, what he can't do and what he doesn't do.

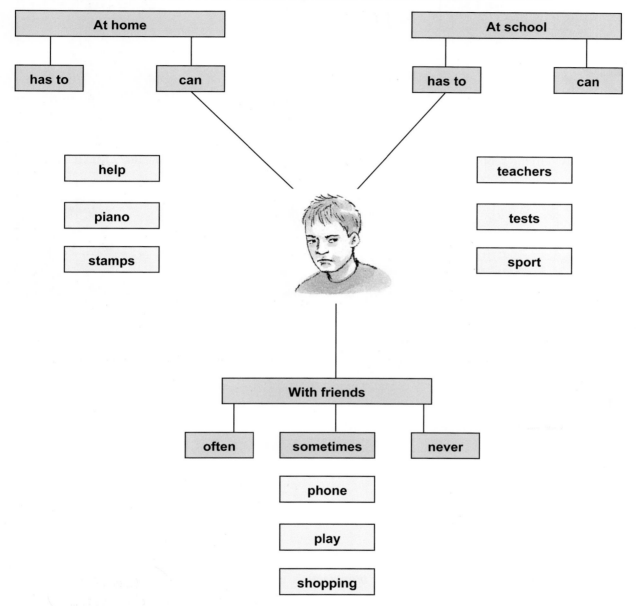

This is Brian's life:
At home he ...

Illustration: **Constanze Schargan**, Berlin

Hamster Rob is watching the Summer family

Look at the pictures. What can Hamster Rob see? What are the Summers doing? What are Hamster Rob's questions? Use the present progressive.

Jessica – not / clean – my cage / She – tidy – living room

Luke – not / feed – me / He – lay – table

Mrs Summer – kitchen / What – she – do? / Make – cake?

Oh! Mr Summer – make – mess! Now Mr Summer and Mrs Summer – argue

Look! The guests – come / They – bring – lots of presents for Jessica and Luke

Jessica and Luke – look at the presents / They – not / look at me

You can start like this:

I'm sitting here in my cage. I can see Jessica. Jessica …

Food and drink

Write a short text (6 sentences) about what you eat and drink every day.

Write what you always / sometimes / … have for breakfast, lunch or dinner.

Write what you like or don't like.

What's your favourite food? What's your favourite drink?

You can start like this:

I always have … for breakfast. …

Illustrationen: **Constanze Schargan**, Berlin (oben); **Katharina Wieker**, Berlin (unten: Food and drink)

Mrs Summer's e-mail

Read Jessica's e-mail. Now write Mrs Summer's e-mail. She is worried. She asks about Luke's leg. She wants to know more about Andrea's friend Susanne, about the farm, about the river, the bridge, the tower and the old box.

From:	JessicaSummer@hotmail.co.uk
To:	
CC:	
Subject:	

Hi Mum, hi Dad,

Yesterday we went to a small village near Neuss. Andrea's friend Susanne lives there on a farm with her parents. The village doesn't have a train station, so we went by bus. It wasn't far to walk from the bus station to the farm. It's a beautiful farm. There is a river, a small bridge and an old tower. Susanne showed us the tower and we explored the place. Andrea found a big box. When Susanne and I opened the box we saw lots of old toys. Susanne took four little boats from the box so each of us had a boat. We took them down to the river and played there under the bridge for a long time. Luke wasn't careful when he climbed on the bridge. He hurt his leg and cried in pain. I touched his leg, but he didn't like that so we put cold water on it. Then we went back to the farm house. Luke smiled again when he saw the big chocolate cake on the table. We all had a piece of it – it was great. It's six o'clock now. Aunt Jane is making dinner. I'm looking forward to it because Aunt Jane always makes really good food.

I hope everything is OK with you.

Love, Jessica

You can start like this:

Hi Jessica, hi Luke, …

My new friends

Write a short text about your friends at your new school.

where   name   how old

he/she has got …   his/her parents

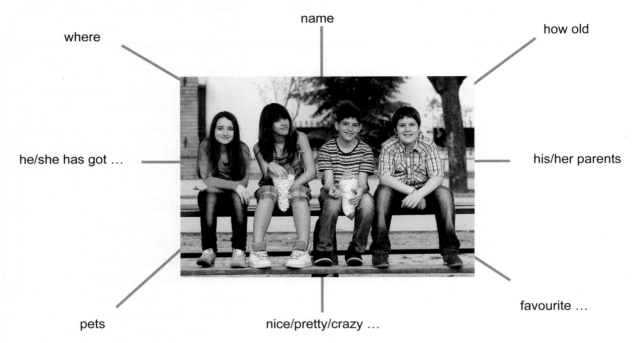

pets   nice/pretty/crazy …   favourite …

You can start like this:

My new friend is …
She/He is … years old.
I like her/his …

About you and your new school

Write a short text about your new school.

Write: about your new school – about your new form teacher – about your favourite teacher – about your favourite subject – about your timetable (only for one day) – about your new friends.

You can start like this:

My school is … On Monday I have got …

Foto: **Shutterstock.com** (oben: prudkov)

Christopher's day

a) *Match the verbs and the pictures.*

> have breakfast – do his homework – play football – get up – feed his guinea pigs
> go to bed – go to school – come home from school – clean his teeth

get up

b) *Write a text about Christopher's day.*

You can start like this:

Christopher gets up at 7 o'clock. At ... he ...

c) *Now write a text about your day.*

You can start like this:

I get up at 6.30 every day. ...

Illustrationen: **Thomas Andrae**, Hamburg

My weekend

Write a short text about your weekend.

You can use:

play – go – listen to – read – clean – sleep – get up – watch – feed – help – …

You can start like this:

Every weekend I get up …
First I …
I like …

An e-mail to …

Write an e-mail to an English friend. Write about your hobbies and sports and ask him/her what he/she does.

You can start like this:

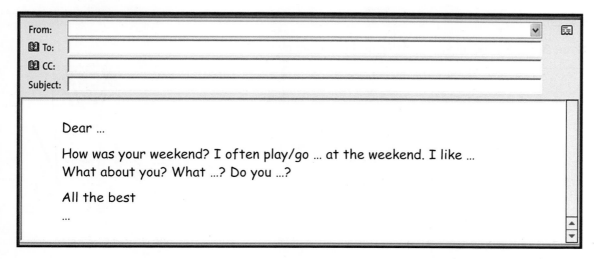

A letter to …

You want more information about one of these three clubs.

The Wizards' Computer Club

Patrick's Dancing School

Cabot Sports Club

- Where …
- When …
- Can I …
- Have you got …
- How much …

Write a letter to one of these clubs. Tell them about yourself (name, address, phone number, hobbies, …) and ask them questions.

You can start like this:

> Dear Cabot Sports Club
>
> My name is … I'm … years old. I like …
>
> Can you tell me …?

Getting ready for Christina's party

Christina is getting ready for her birthday party. Her mum is helping her.

Look at the pictures and write what they are doing.

You can start like this:

It's 10 o'clock on Saturday morning. Christina and her mum are …

An invitation to a party

You want to have a party.

Write an invitation to a friend. Think of the time, place, what party it is, …

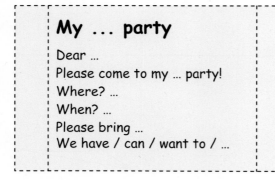

My … party

Dear …
Please come to my … party!
Where? …
When? …
Please bring …
We have / can / want to / …

Birthday?
Halloween?
Sleepover?
Fancy-dress?
Barbecue?
Disco?

Illustrationen: **Thomas Andrae**, Hamburg

Cornelsen

A great party – a terrible party

Last week you went to a party. It was a great party (or it was a terrible party).

Write an e-mail to an English friend and tell him/her about that party.

You can start like this: Last week I went to my friend ...'s party. There was ...

Words you can use:

food – drink – music – (to) dance – (to) laugh

These pictures may help you:

A visitor from England

A friend from England is coming to stay with you for a week in Germany. Maybe he/she wants to see your school too.

Write an e-mail to him/her about Germany, where you live in Germany and about your school. What activities can you do together? What is different in Germany? Complete the mind map first.

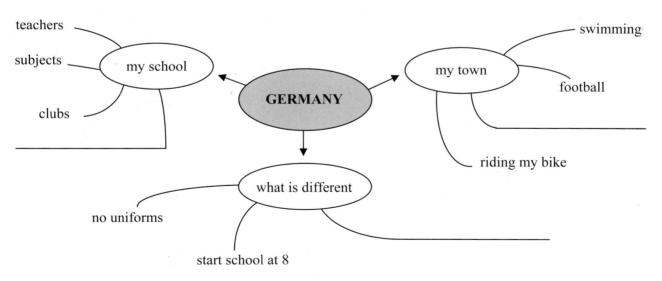

Illustrationen: **Thomas Andrae**, Hamburg

Where German kids live

An English school magazine is doing a report on German kids. They asked your class for some information.

Write an article and tell them something about the place where you live. Is it interesting or boring? Why?

You can use these words:

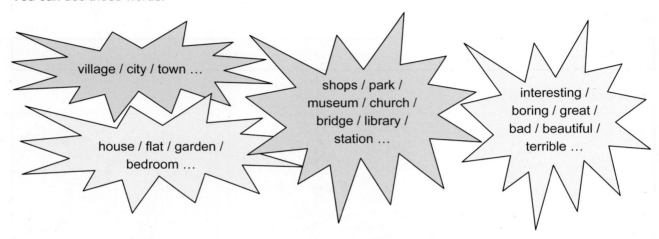

village / city / town …

house / flat / garden / bedroom …

shops / park / museum / church / bridge / library / station …

interesting / boring / great / bad / beautiful / terrible …

An interesting place

Imagine your English partner school wants to write an article about interesting places in Germany in their school magazine.

Think of an interesting place. Then write an e-mail to your English friend and tell him/her about that place.

You can start like this:

Dear …
Last month I went to … It was great because …

Here are some ideas:

Where was it?
What was it?
How did you get there?
What did you do?
Why did you like it?
What was the best thing about it?

Sally's School of Dancing

You want to have dancing lessons. Fill in this form.

Welcome to Sally's School of Dancing		
Family name		First name
Date of birth		Place of birth
Your address		
house number	name of street	name of city
Course ❑ break dance ❑ ballet ❑ African ❑ salsa ❑ jazz		
What day of the week do you want to dance?		
Your phone number		Your e-mail address
City, date		Signature

Join our club

There are British kids at your school and they can go to one of your school clubs.

Help them and explain one club in English for them:

Der Fotoklub

- über Kameras lernen
- nette Leute treffen
- jeden Donnerstag
- Raum 8
- bring deine Kamera

Der Musikklub
Gitarre, Klavier oder Klarinette spielen
mit anderen Musik machen
für die Vorstellung proben
jeden Dienstag
– im Musikraum –

Write about one club in English. You can use the words in the boxes:

We learn about play/rehearse/…	You can make/meet/come/…	We meet … in … / every …

A special day

Write an e-mail to an English friend about a special day. Write at least six sentences. You can use:

From:

To:

CC:

Subject:

- Last … / On Saturday / …   – was … a day

- In the morning/afternoon …   – I was … / I went to … / I had …

- First … / Then …   – I/We played/saw/watched …

- It really was …   – a … day/trip

You can start like this:
Dear (Peter) …, …

At Bristol Zoo

This is the core of a story.

Add words, places, times from the box to these sentences. Write a really interesting story. Think of a nice title!

You can start your story like this: Yesterday my best friend and I went to the zoo ...

Use these words for your story:

We went to the zoo.
We like animals.
We went with my parents.
We saw animals.
I liked the elephants.
We had an ice cream.
We were tired.
We went home.
It was a ... day.

a lot of	after four hours

interesting	very much

in Bristol	chocolate

best	by bus

after some time	great

Cabot Tower

Write a short text about Cabot Tower for a poster presentation. Use these notes:

- Cabot Tower / 32.4 m high – on a hill / near Bristol Harbour
- the tower / over 100 years old – John Cabot / to America / in 1497
- Cabot / with his ship / to Newfoundland / in North America
- the name / his ship / Matthew
- Cabot Tower / from many parts of the city

Use the correct form of these verbs:

be (4 x) – go – come – can see

Fotos: **Shutterstock.com** (oben: Dariush M; unten: Bob Cheung)

A bike trip

Last summer Amy went on a bike trip with her friends.

Look at the pictures and write down what Amy and her friends did and what the weather was like. Write at least two sentences for each picture.

A letter to a friend

a) *Imagine you went to Austria with your parents last summer. Write a letter to your English friend and tell him or her about your holiday. The pictures can help you. Write at least eight sentences.*

Write about
- where you were
- how you got there
- what the weather was like
- what you did there
- what you liked / didn't like

Start like this:

Dear …
Thank you for your postcard. We were in Austria and we really had a great time. We went there by …

b) *Now you. Write a letter about your holidays. Write at least eight sentences.*

Illustrationen: **Katharina Wieker**, Berlin

A day out

Write about a trip to a zoo or an imaginary trip[1] to Longleat Safari Park. You can use the poster. Write at least eight sentences.

Write – where you were
– who you were with
– what animals you saw/watched there
– what other activities you did
– what you liked best

Use words like

First … / Later … / After …
Before … / … and / … because

A day out at Longleat

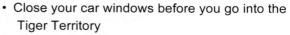

* Discover the adventure castle with its bridges, nets and slides[2] – things you can climb through
* Find your way in the Longleat Hedge Maze[3]
* Go on a Safari boat trip and watch the sea lions and pelicans
* Be very close to rabbits, guinea pigs, chinchillas, tortoises and other pet animals in the pet corner
* Have great fun on your drive through the monkey jungle

* Close your car windows before you go into the Tiger Territory
* Come to our Deer Park, the only place where you can feed the animals
* Watch the zebras, giraffes, camels and rhinos grazing the grasslands of the East Africa Reserve
* Enjoy a ride on the Longleat Railway

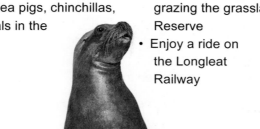

---

[1] imaginary trip *Fantasiereise* – [2] slide *Rutsche* – [3] maze *Irrgarten*

A letter to Hi!

Write a letter to teen magazine Hi! Start and finish your letter in a good way. Write at least eight sentences.

Write about – how much pocket money you get
– what you buy with it
– how much you save
– what you save your money for

Caernarfon Castle

a) *Find a topic sentence. Then write a good paragraph.*

one of the biggest castles in Wales

13 towers

Edward I built the castle

lots of old things in the towers

Caernarfon – nice town – walk around – after visit to castle

walk from one tower to the other on the castle wall

b) *Now you.*

Is there a special place you like or you have been to?

Write an e-mail (four sentences) to an English friend about it. Find a good topic sentence, then write

- what is special about it
- where it is
- what you can do there

You can start like this:

Dear ...,

An e-mail to a friend

Write an e-mail to a friend in England about an interesting place in Germany. Write eight sentences.

Write
- where the place is
- when you went there
- what you can do there
- what is good/interesting/boring
- why you like it

Foto: **Shutterstock.com** (Oliver Hoffmann)

Caius' lucky day

Write this story about Caius, the little dog. It happened 2000 years ago in Pompeii.

Early in the afternoon Livia, Julia and Felix were playing with Caius, Julia's little dog. Suddenly Julia saw …

ashes (Asche) and stones

run – shout

houses – fall down

on the beach – look for Caius

very sad

stone on the ground – hole – sound

pick up

Illustrationen: **Katharina Wieker**, Berlin

Dan and Jo went sea-kayaking

Dan and Jo are visiting their mother in New Zealand.

Write this story about the two boys. Use the simple past.

Last Thursday – Dan and Jo –
beach with their mother.
The boys – want to go –
on a sea-kayaking tour

Dan and Jo – get into their kayak.
Tour guide – Tim.
Tim – explain – the tour

The boys – paddle – round a rock.
Suddenly Dan – shout

The boys – paddle –
out to the open sea.
three dolphins

dolphins – very close
Jo – camera – take photos

boys – paddle back – tell mum:
'Mum, it was really great. We've
never seen dolphins before!'

My last trip

Write a report (about 60 words) about your last trip with your class or family or friends.

Say
- when you went
- where you went
- who went with you
- what the weather was like
- if something special happened
- what the trip was like

Illustrationen: **Katharina Wieker**, Berlin

A holiday postcard

You want to write a postcard to your friend Paul Wells in Edinburgh. Choose one of the postcards and tell him:

- where you are
- where you are staying
- what you did yesterday
- what you want to do today
- what the weather is like
- how long you are there

Write 6 or more sentences and an ending into the postcard.

Dear Paul,

Paul Wells
3, Arnhem Drive
Edinburgh EH2 2DG

An e-mail to Germany

Simon is an English boy from Bristol. In his holidays he was in Scotland at an international music camp. He met Kai, a boy from Munich, Germany. At the end of September he writes an e-mail to Kai.

Er schreibt,
– wann er wieder mit der Schule begann und was es Neues aus der Schule gibt,
– dass er das *international music camp* super fand,
– dass er viel gelernt hat,
– dass er hofft, mal wieder in ein *music camp* gehen zu können.

Er fragt Kai,
– ob es Kai im *music camp* auch gefallen hat,
– ob er wieder mal nach Großbritannien kommen möchte,
– ob er viel Englisch in Schottland gelernt hat,
– was er in den letzten zwei Wochen seiner Ferien gemacht hat.

Er bittet Kai,
– ihm etwas aus der deutschen Schule zu erzählen.

Write a beginning and an ending.

Start like this:

An article for the school magazine

You are writing an article for the school magazine about the school garden project.

Use the following key words and write at least eight complete sentences.

1 topic – school garden
2 old garden – not nice
3 but! – no money
4 make and sell cakes – school – Bristol Market
5 need help – Mr Hull from the flower shop – parents
6 end of the project – presentation – parents
7 cakes and drink – say thank you

You can start like this:

The school garden
I'm writing about our school project. Our topic was …

A letter to Ian

You and your friends went to a fun run last week.

Write a letter to your friend Ian in Glasgow and tell him about the fun run. Use the flyer below.

Write
– why you think a fun run is a good idea
– who or what the fun run was for
– about your sponsor: Who was it? How did you find him/her? How much money did he/she give you for each mile?
– who you ran with
– how many miles you ran together
– what you liked best
– an end

You can start like this:

> Bristol, 1st June
>
> Dear Ian,
>
> I went to a fun run last week, …

Animal Helpline Bristol – Fun run for young and old

- Come and join our fun run in Bristol on 23rd May, 9 am – 3 pm.
- Find a sponsor for your miles and run as long as you like.
- Come with all your friends and run 21 miles together.
- Every mile helps an animal.
- The money goes directly to Animal Helpline.

See you on 23rd May!!!

Foto: **Shutterstock.com** (Boguslaw Mazur)

An e-mail to the Shocking Smoothies Team

You have read an article on the website of Cotham School about their smoothies bar. You like the idea and want to find out more about the smoothies project, because you and your friends want to open a smoothies bar at your school too.

Write an e-mail to the Shocking Smoothies team and ask for details. The notes will help you. Don't forget to write a beginning and an ending.

> **e-mail to Cotham School:**
> - read article on the internet
> - like your idea
> - open smoothies bar at our school
> - many questions
> - how – start?
> - students – how many?
> - price?
> - problems?
> - ask head teacher – before you started?
> - glasses?
> - send – recipe

Boring!

Tim's homework was: 'Write a story about a boring Saturday afternoon'.

Can you write Tim's story?

Use simple past forms.

Use time phrases too: First, then, after that, an hour later, …

Ideas: football, watch kids, weather, rainy, help mum, clean bike, tidy room, wash car, …

Birthday party at the Roman Baths

Sara had her birthday party at the Roman baths. Sue was one of her guests.

Look at the pictures and write a text for Sue's diary. Say what you liked and what was funny. Use some of the linking words and adjectives in the box.

Linking words:	**Adjectives:**
at two o'clock – a few minutes – later – suddenly – then – next – so – but	funny – intersting – nice – great – amazing – beautiful – best – difficult – easy – exciting – fantastic – favourite – happy

meet – Sara's house

cycle to

man – tell plans for the afternoon

bring – Roman clothes put on – laugh

have – drinks, …

go round – look at

make sandals

cycle home

Dear diary,

Today I went to Sara's birthday party. We met …

Illustrationen: **Constanze Schargan**, Berlin

An e-mail about your last holiday

Write an e-mail to your penfriend Steve about your last holiday.

Write a beginning and an ending.

Tell him:
- when you went
- where you went
- who went with you
- where you stayed
- what you did
- what you liked about it
- what you didn't like about it

Use 'little' words from the list to make your sentences.

and – so – but – too – also

An e-mail about you

Write an e-mail to your friend (about 60 words). Write about

- what you do in your free time
- what your favourite hobby is
- one or two things about your favourite hobby

The pictures can help you.

Illustrationen: **Katharina Wieker**, Berlin

Millie, Minnie and Molly

Compare Millie, Minnie and Molly Muddles. Write five sentences or more. Use: young, old, big, small, long, short, dark, funny

Ideas: Who is younger/bigger than the others? Who is the oldest? Who has got the longest hair, the darkest hair? Who is the funniest?

Millie, 4   Minnie, 2   Molly, 6

Korky

a) *Your pet dog Korky is ill. Write an e-mail about Korky to a friend. Link two sentences with a linking word from the left or the middle.*

	My dog Korky is eleven years old.		He's my best friend.
	I'm not very happy at the moment.		Korky is ill.
	He must be hungry.	but	He doesn't eat his food.
When	I come home from school.	and	We usually go to the park.
After	I took him to the park yesterday.	because	He just sat under a tree and slept.
	I feed him.	so	He usually wants to play with me.
	He's always a happy dog.		He's very quiet now.
	We're worried about him.		Maybe we'll take him to the animal clinic tomorrow.

_____

_____

_____

b) *Now write at least three more sentences about Korky. Use a linking word from* **a)** *in each sentence.*

_____

_____

_____

Illustrationen: **Roland Beier**, Berlin

A visit to Germany

Your friend Steve from England is going to visit you for a week. He has never been to Germany.

Write him an e-mail and tell him what activities you want to do with him. What interesting things are there to see or do where you live? Write at least eight sentences.

The pictures and the box will give you some ideas.

- Are you interested in ...?
- Where I live there are lots of ...
- We have a very good ...
- I'd like to show you ...
- It's really interesting/beautiful/great/...
- Do you like ...?

You can start like this:

Dear Steve
I'm happy that you're going to visit me. ... is a great place. ...

Yesterday ...

Think about yesterday and write a short text about what you did. Here are some ideas.

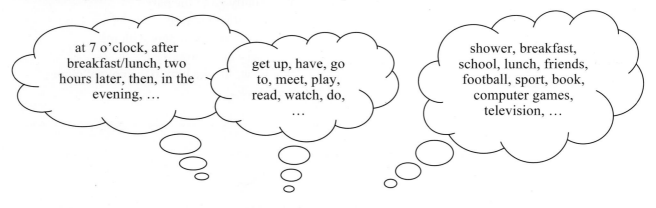

at 7 o'clock, after breakfast/lunch, two hours later, then, in the evening, ...

get up, have, go to, meet, play, read, watch, do, ...

shower, breakfast, school, lunch, friends, football, sport, book, computer games, television, ...

You can start like this: Yesterday I got up at 7 o'clock. I had a shower and then I had ...

Illustrationen: **Katharina Wieker**, Berlin

Money problems

Look at Holly and Dylan's problems below.

*Write a letter to **one of them** about what he/she can do.*

Holly's problem
- Mother always chooses her clothes
- Friends have got nicer clothes
- Not enough pocket money
- Spends all of it on mobile phone

Dylan's problem
- Pocket money: only £ 3 a month
- Lives in small village
- No jobs
- Parents haven't got a lot of money

You can start like this:

Dear ...

I can see you've got a problem with ... . Why do you ...? You can ... . Why don't you ...?

It's a good idea to ...

An awful day ...

Your friend Susan from England sends you an e-mail and asks you how you are. You had a very bad day yesterday.

Write back to her and tell her about it. Here are some ideas.

- late for school
- teacher angry
- difficult homework
- room a mess
- Mum/Dad very angry
- cat disappear
- ...

You can start like this:

Dear Susan,

I'm fine, but I had a very bad day yesterday. ...

A baby cat

Your friend Vanessa from England sends you this e-mail:

From:
To:
CC:
Subject:

Dear ...

How are you? I'm fine, but something strange happened yesterday. When I came home in the evening, I heard a strange noise from the garden. I went outside and found this baby cat under a bush! It's really sweet. I took it inside because I couldn't see its mother or any other cats. Now I really don't know what to do! I know you've got a cat at home, so can you tell me what I can do?
Please write soon

Love,

Vanessa

Write back to her (at least eight sentences) and tell her what to do. Here are some ideas.

keep it warm – no milk – call the RSPCA – be careful – keep it in the house –
cat food – ask friends – look for its mother

My pet

Write at least eight sentences about your pet or your dream pet.

Write
    – what pet it is
    – its name
    – how old it is
    – what it looks like
    – where it lives (sleeps)
    – what you like about it and why
    – how often you have to feed it
    – when you feed it and what you give it
    – what it can do or likes to do

The future

The English magazine Hi! asked its readers what they think the future will look like.

Write a letter to them (at least eight sentences) and tell them what you think. The pictures will give you some ideas.

... more ideas?

You can start like this:

Dear Hi!

I think a lot of things will be different in the future. ...

Illustrationen: **Katharina Wieker**, Berlin

My best / My worst weekend trip

Write a text about a very good or a very bad weekend trip. Write at least eight sentences.

Think of the following points:

– Where did you go?
– What was the weather like?

– Who went with you?
– What happened? Why was it good/bad?

The pictures and the box will give you some ideas.

rainy – sunny –
too late – have fun –
bad food – exciting –
accident – nice people –
no money – photos –
never again!

David's accident

Look at the pictures and tell the story of David's accident. Write a short text of at least eight sentences.

The box will give you some ideas.

You can start like this:

It was Saturday morning. David ...

bike – go swimming – friend Alan – shout 'hi' –
car in front – hit the car – fall – leg hurt –
paramedics – hospital – leg broken – stay in hospital

Illustrationen: **Katharina Wieker**, Berlin

Tom's birthday party

Christine is writing an e-mail to her friend Sally about what was happening when she arrived late for Tom's birthday party last week.

Look at the picture and write her e-mail. Write at least eight sentences.

You can start like this:

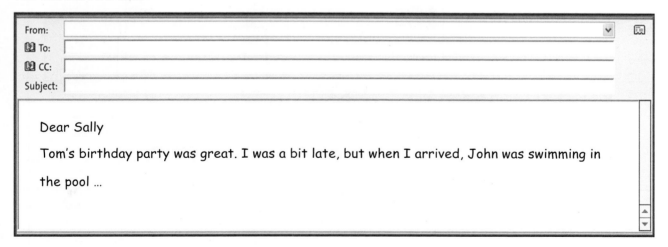

From:

To:

CC:

Subject:

Dear Sally

Tom's birthday party was great. I was a bit late, but when I arrived, John was swimming in

the pool ...

How to find me

Your friend Michael from England is in Germany, and he wants to come and visit you for a day. But you're waiting for another friend, so you can't go and meet him at the station.

Look at the map and describe the way from the station to your house in an e-mail to Michael. Write at least eight sentences.

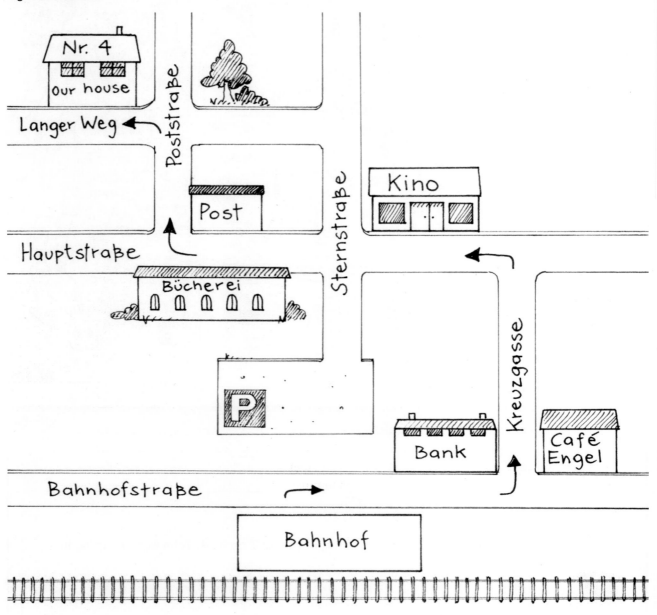

You can start like this:

Dear Michael
It's quite easy to find me. When you come out of the station, turn …

Illustrationen: **Katharina Wieker**, Berlin

Mrs Lazybones' day

Mrs Lazybones had a great day yesterday. Write what she did yesterday.

At nine o'clock – be in bed

At nine o'clock Mrs Lazybones was still in bed.

Then – have breakfast

Then _____

_____

After breakfast – have a shower

_____

_____

At eleven o'clock –
play with dog

_____

_____

An hour later –
read a magazine

_____

_____

In the afternoon –
go shopping

_____

_____

When she came home –
call a friend

_____

_____

At eight o'clock –
listen to music

_____

_____

After that –
watch a film

_____

_____

Illustrationen: **Constanze Schargan**, Berlin

Greetings from London

You are in London with your family for some days and are enjoying the beautiful city. Before your holidays, your English teacher asked you to write an e-mail to him/her.

Write this e-mail (60–80 words) and tell your teacher about your stay in London.

Write – where you are
– what you like best
– what's special about the city
– about the weather
– how you like your stay
– about the things you did yesterday
– which sights you are going to visit next

Give your e-mail a good beginning and end.

Remember: Make your sentences more interesting by using adjectives and time phrases.

An e-mail about a school trip

Your German school has got a partner school in Canada. You often write e-mails to each other about what happens at your school. Today you want to tell the Canadian students about your last school trip.

Write about

– where you went, your journey, where you stayed
– what it was like, the people, what you were allowed / not allowed to do, the food, your teachers

Use the simple past.

You can start like this:

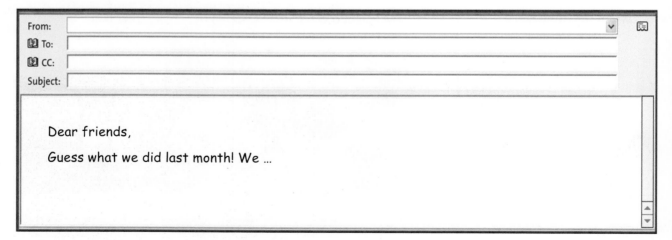

From:	
To:	
CC:	
Subject:	

Dear friends,

Guess what we did last month! We …

A letter from Asif

You and your class went on a five-day school trip to Berlin. Your English friend Asif knew about it and has sent you this letter:

> Dear …
>
> How are you? I hope you liked my photos and the information about 'my London'. It's a really great and a very intersting city. Please come and visit me one day. How was your trip to Berlin? Is Berlin as interesting as London? What did you like best? Did you take lots of photos? Please write about your time in Berlin.
> Give my love to your parents.
>
> Love,
> Asif

Write an e-mail to Asif and answer his questions. Tell him what you did in Berlin. The following photos and notes will help you. Write 60–80 words.

Berlin: – big / very interesting
   – River Spree
   – lots of sights, e.g.:

Brandenburg Gate:
– over 200 years old

Reichstag building:
– near Brandenburg Gate
– seat of the German parliament

TV Tower:
– at Alexanderplatz
– about 365 metres high

Kurfürstendamm:
– famous shopping street
– 3.5 km long

Fotos: **Shutterstock.com** (oben li.: Ognivenko, oben re.: Stefan Delle, unten li.: Vitaly Goncharov, unten re.: Kaspars Grinvalds)

A bad start to a nice day

Look at the pictures and use the words to write a text in the simple past about Michael's day. Use time phrases and linking words to make your story more interesting. Write about 80–100 words.

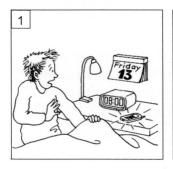

Michael – wake up – late

get dressed – run to bus stop; too late

hungry – go to bakery – buy sandwich

phone Mum – ask her

Mum – take to school

teacher – wait; classmates – in bus

go on trip to coast

sit on beach – warm – sunny; go swimming

A report about a day out

Your school has got a partner school in Bristol. Your class has started an internet blog to tell the English pupils about the highlights of your school year.

Today you have to write a report for the blog. You can write about an (imaginary) class trip / your project week or any other interesting event that has taken place at your school. Write 80–100 words.

Write about
– what/when/where/why
– who went with you
– what you liked about it
– what was special about it
– what you learned

Remember: Give your report a structure (beginning/middle/end).
Start a new paragraph for each new idea.
Start each paragraph with a topic sentence.

Illustrationen: **Katharina Wieker**, Berlin

An exciting day on the river

Last summer Jordan, Robert and Robert's uncle went canoeing on Grand River together.

Look at the pictures and write their story. Remember: A story should have a beginning, a middle and an end. Try to make your story interesting with adjectives (e.g. quick/scared/young/cold), linking words and time phrases (e.g. suddenly / some minutes later / after that).

Sunny day – Jordan, Robert, Robert's uncle – go canoeing – Grand River

Loud noise – shout: 'Help!' Girl – hold on to a rock

Boat – try to get to the girl Water – wild

Robert – call police

Find a place – leave the boat

Run back – girl Robert – shout

Loud noise – above their heads Helicopter – ladder Man – climb down – get the girl

Next day – article – newspaper

Illustrationen: **Katharina Wieker**, Berlin

A letter to a teen magazine

Alyssa has sent this letter to a teen magazine.

Read and answer it. Tell Alyssa what you are allowed or not allowed to do. Write about 80 words.

Dear Reader

I've got big problems with my parents at the moment. I'm not allowed to do anything! I'm not allowed to watch TV or use my computer after nine o'clock on school nights. My mom always complains about my music and I can't play loud music. I'm not allowed to colour my hair or have piercings. I can't buy my own clothes. Last week I did badly in a test and now I'm not allowed to go out for a week. I'm grounded. It's so unfair! Am I the only one with strict parents? Or are there people out there who've got the same problems? Please write to me.

Your unhappy Alyssa

You could start like this:

Dear Alyssa
I've got big problems with my parents at the moment too …

OR

I don't have any problems with my parents. They aren't too strict …

Magazines

Your partner school's newspaper wants to tell its readers about the kind of magazines that Germans students read and if there are students who don't read magazines.

Write about your favourite magazine. Write about 80–100 words.

Write – the name of the magazine
  – what it costs and who pays for it
  – how often / where you buy it
  – about the topics in the magazine
  – why you like it
  – which articles you like and why
  – …

OR

Write why you don't read magazines. Write about 80–100 words.

Write – about your reasons (too expensive / no time / boring / …)
  – what other things you read (newspaper / articles on the internet / …)
  – if you think it's a problem not to read magazines

A diary about our trip to London

In her summer holidays, Sue spends four days in London with her parents and her brother. You are Sue and write your diary about your first day. Write down what you liked ☺ and what you didn't like ☹. Write about your feelings too. Write about 100 words.

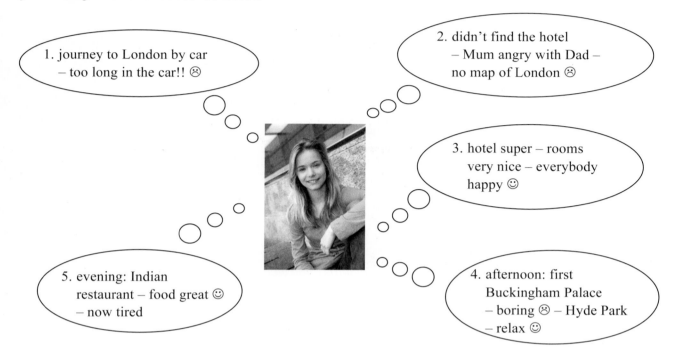

1. journey to London by car
   – too long in the car!! ☹

2. didn't find the hotel
   – Mum angry with Dad –
   no map of London ☹

3. hotel super – rooms
   very nice – everybody
   happy ☺

5. evening: Indian
   restaurant – food great ☺
   – now tired

4. afternoon: first
   Buckingham Palace
   – boring ☹ – Hyde Park
   – relax ☺

You can start like this:

> Dear diary,
>
> Mum, Dad, Ron and I started our journey to London this morning …

What an event!

It was just great! Write about a football match, another sports event or a concert you played in, watched or you read about. Write a report (about 60–70 words) on this event. In your report answer these questions:

– What event was it?
– Who took part in it?
– Where was it?
– When was it?
– Why did you like it?

A report for the school magazine

Together with his school orchestra, Leo went on a school trip to the 'Music for Youth Festival' in Birmingham. There he met Katrina. After his trip he wrote a report about it for his school magazine. Write Leo's report. Use the following ideas:

– Write about making friends on a school trip.
– Say who you are and what instrument you play (for how long – who started to teach you – where do you play now).
– Say what you did at the festival and how you felt.
– Tell the readers about your new friend Katrina (instrument – who taught her – about her father – where she goes to school).
– Say how you are going to keep in touch with her.
– Tell your readers what they can do to meet new friends.

A day out to the Lowry

Imagine you are a student at a school in Leeds. Yesterday you went on a day out to the Lowry in Manchester. You write a report about your visit to the Lowry for the school magazine.

In your report answer these questions:

– **Who?**	students of Form 7 LM
– **What event was it?**	a day out
– **Where?**	to the Lowry in Manchester – building amazing
– **When?**	February 25th, from 10 am to 2 pm – by train – nice walk to the museum – sunshine
– **Why?**	do a presentation about the famous painter L. S. Lowry, find out about him, collect information, copy one of Lowry's paintings
– **How?**	very interesting, different games and activities around the paintings, some students: design their own postcards
– **What happened?**	a boy – touch painting – alarm – police – not arrest

© 2014 Cornelsen Schulverlage GmbH, Berlin. Alle Rechte vorbehalten.

Correcting mistakes

Read the following text carefully and find the twelve mistakes. Then rewrite the text.

About my favourite star – a quiz

My favourite star is a man. He is born in england in 1982. When he was five years old he became his first guitar of his father. He has started to play and soon he was quite good. He learned to sing too. His friends liked his music. Very often asked they him to play on partys. When he was 18 he played his first concert and at the age of 22 released he his first CD. It was a sucess. It was selled over 500,000 time.

Can you guess who it is?

New editors for TEEN MAGAZINE

Dear readers of TEEN MAGAZINE,

We want to start new sections for **TEEN MAGAZINE** and are looking for motivated young editors. You'll find some ideas for a new section here:

> cycling – quiz page – new games – computer world – Canada – holidays

Are you interested or have you got any other ideas? If so, please send an e-mail to us: brandon@teenmagazine.cim

You want to start a new section for TEEN MAGAZINE. Write an e-mail to Brandon with the following information:

- write about yourself and what you think about TEEN MAGAZINE
- write about the section you would like to open and say why you are interested in it (you may choose from the box or add a new idea)
- give details about your ideas for this section and about the first article you want to write (possible articles, …)
- give your full name, address and phone number

Write about 150 words.

Foto: **Shutterstock.com** (Olga Miltsova)

Writing better sentences

The text below is boring. Write it again. Add words and phrases from the grey box to make it more interesting.

> after a few minutes – almost – loud – loudly – on the lake – really – so – soon – strange –
> strong – suddenly – then – under the trees – very – yesterday

> … it was a hot day … I went to the park lake. / I sat down … and … I was asleep. / I had a … dream. /
> I was in a boat … / It was dark and … quiet. / … I found that the boat had a hole. / … it was … full of
> water. / I felt … scared. / … I heard a … voice. / Somebody shouted my name … / A … hand grabbed my
> arm. 'Here you are, asleep!' said Dad.

The schools' cup final

a) *A young reporter is writing a short report about Nick's school match for a newspaper. How can you make the report better? What should stay in the report? Mark the sentences blue. What should the reporter leave out? Mark the sentences red.*

Rosehill Park School played against St. Joseph's Catholic School in Bridgeford last Saturday. It was cold for the time of the year. There wasn't much sun and there were some dark clouds. It was the schools' cup final. The match started ten minutes late.

Both teams made a fast start. The first goal was scored in the 29th minute by St. Joseph's captain, Luke Newman. At half-time the score was still 0–1 for St. Joseph's. It rained a bit in the break. In an exciting second half, Rosehill's captain Nick Scott was fouled. He took the penalty and equalized. A second goal for Rosehill Park was scored in the 89th minute, again by Nick Scott. St. Joseph's were tired and made mistakes. Their team captain argued with the goalkeeper.

The final score was 2–1 for Rosehill, who were the stronger team. Nick Scott's mum is going to buy him a new football. The cup was presented by footballer Michael Ashley, a TV celebrity. He had a bad cold. The match was watched by a large crowd of students, parents and teachers.

b) *Now write the final report.*

Foto: **Shutterstock.com** (Viorel Sima)

The camping trip

a) *Here's the beginning of a story about a camping trip.*

It was a hot week at the beginning of August. Jordan and his dad wanted to do a camping trip together, because they both enjoyed climbing and looking for animals. So they went to Algonquin Park for a few days. Jordan's cousin Dave went with them.

How can the story continue? In your exercise book, write the middle of the story in the simple past. Use these notes, or use your own ideas.

The first night – all tired – sleep well / Next morning Dave – get up early – walk – wash room on campground / Jordan and dad – wait a long time, but Dave – not come / Jordan and dad – worried – look for Dave – not there / Jordan and dad – go – wash room / On the way there – find – Dave's towel and soap – path / Suddenly – feel scared / accident – bear?

b) *Think of an exciting or interesting ending. Maybe you can think of a good explanation why Dave had disappeared. Write the ending and give the story a title.*

Organizing ideas

a) *Read a part of Robert's e-mail to Cem. First, mark the sentence parts that give answers to the '5 Ws' and How?*

I must tell you about our last big trip. We went to Vancouver on the west coast. It's a long way from Toronto so we can't go there often. I've only been there twice. The last time was in August, in the school holidays. It's too far to drive there, so we – my parents, me and my grandma from Toronto – went by plane. Grandma was more excited than I was!
We went to visit family – and to enjoy the city, of course. My Uncle Joe, Aunt Stacey and two cousins live near Vancouver. We saw all the city sights – Stanley Park and the Aquarium …,

b) *Now write down the information in the e-mail that answers the questions:*

What? _____

When? _____

Where? _____

Who? _____

Why? _____

How? _____

Correcting your text

a) *Your friend's homework was: 'Write a short biography of a star.' He/She wrote about Robbie Williams. Read the text carefully and mark the mistakes in red.*

© 2014 Cornelsen Schulverlage GmbH, Berlin.
Alle Rechte vorbehalten.

ROBBIE WILLIAMS

Robbie Williams is born on 13 February, 1974 in Newcastle-under-Lyme, UK. His singing carreer started with the band Take That. He played with them
5 for five years. The bands' success was huge. You could hear in the radio their songs. The others in the group said that Williams did not work hardly enough. He choosed to leave the band. In 1995 he has become a solo singer.
10 He released his first album in 1997.
He has sold more then 50 million albums and 15 million singles too. In the UK he has sold more albums as any other solo singer in history. Williams has been popular all over the world. But he hasn't been so successful in North America. His best album in the US – 'Angels'– was only number 41
15 in the charts.

INFO BOX!

When Robbie Williams announced his World Tour for 2006 1.6 million tickets were sold in one day! This gave Williams a place in the Guiness Book of Records!

b) *There are ten mistakes. Where are they? Write the line numbers and correct the mistakes.*

	Mistake on line	**Correct**
Wrong spelling (2):	_____	_____
	_____	_____
Wrong word:	_____	_____
Wrong preparation:	_____	_____
Wrong tense (2):	_____	_____
	_____	_____
Wrong irregular verb form:	_____	_____
Wrong word order (SPO):	_____	_____
Wrong adverb form:	_____	_____
Wrong possessive form:	_____	_____

c) *Extra – How would you improve the text? Tick (✓) the boxes.*

I would …
☐ use paragraphs.
☐ use linking words (and, so, but, when, although).
☐ add a few adverbs (very, really).
☐ add time phrases (every day, soon after that).

d) *Write the text again with your corrections from b) and your changes in c).*

A postcard from London

Read Niklas postcard.

Dear Thomas, I have to go now, we need to catch the bus to our youth hostel. But today was a brilliant day. We went to Madame Tussauds in the morning. We saw the London Eye just a few minutes ago. In the afternoon we were at Buckingham Palace. Madame Tussauds was very expensive. The food in the hostel is OK. I didn't see the Queen at the palaye. How is your leg? I'm sharing a room with Simon and Lukas. The bus trip here was very long, we slept on the bus. The weather is fine, so no London rain ☺. Mr Schmidt woke us at 7.30! Too early, I think. I will call you when I am back home, Yours, Niklas

Thomas Evans

34 Owen Street
Carmarthen
SA 34 OJP Carms.
Great Britain

'That's not a good postcard for Thomas,' he thinks, and buys a new one.
He wants to write a better postcard this time.

Can you help Niklas? He already knows what he wants to change:

1 He wants to put the information into the right order.
2 He wants to add more linking words (after, in the morning, in the afternoon, in the evening, because, but, so, and, then, first, when, …).

A letter to a friend

This is part of a letter you got from your English friend Robby.

… I've just tried a new sport – New age kurling. It looks boring, but it's really exciting. What do you do in your free time? Do you do any sports? … Please write back soon. Yours, Robby	

Now write a letter to Robby and tell him about your sports interests or another hobby.

Write at least 60 words. Start and finish your letter in a friendly way.

Write about   – what you do   – what you need   – where you do it
              – why you like it   – when you do it (how often)   – …

Illustration: **Katharina Wieker**, Berlin

Writing a report on your last class trip

a) *What can you remember about your last class trip? Write a report on it for your school's year book. Start collecting information for the '5 Ws' and say how you liked the trip:*

Questions	Information	Order
WHO?		
WHERE? (Where did you go? Where did you stay?)		
WHAT? (What did you do? Did you go on any day trips? Did you play any games? Did you do any sports? …)		
WHEN? (Which month? Time of the year? What was the weather like? …)		
WHY? (What was the aim/reason for your class trip?)		
HOW? (How did you like the trip? What was the atmosphere like in the group?		

b) *Now put your information in a useful order by adding numbers in the third column. Then write the report. Don't forget to link your ideas. When you have finished, read the text again and then find a good title for it.*

Here are some ideas that may help you.

> take the … / go by train, by coach
> stay at a youth hostel / camping site / hotel
> go on day / bicycle trips
> play funny games together
> stay up late
> go for a walk (in the night)
> play table tennis / basketball / football
> organize a disco
> sing together
> have a lot of fun

Talking about oneself – my own biography

a) *Please fill in this questionnaire to collect first ideas for writing your biography.*

Name: _____

Born (when/where): _____

Details about your family

– brothers and sisters, parents: _____

_____

– their ages, jobs, interests: _____

_____

School

– name and place: _____

– classmates and teachers: _____

_____

Hobbies: _____

_____

b) *Now write a proper biography. Write it on an extra piece of paper and decorate it with photos or drawings.*

c) *Use this checklist to improve your text.*

- Is there a paragraph for each new idea?
- Are some sentences too short? Are there enough linking words?
- Would more adjectives or adverbs improve the text?
- Are the beginning and ending interesting?
- Will the rest interest the reader?
- Is there anything that you don't need?
- Have you got any other ideas?

Writing about a star

a) *Read the interview with Lady GaGa. Write down the missing questions.*

Reporter: Hello, _____ ?

Lady GaGa: Fine, thank you.

Reporter: Great. So let's start with the questions.

_____ ?

Lady GaGa: My real name is Stefani Joanne Angelina Germanotta.

Reporter: Oh, that sounds Italian.

_____ ?

Lady GaGa: No, I'm not from Italy. I'm from Yonkers, New York
in the USA. But my parents are Italian Americans.

Reporter: _____ ?

Lady GaGa: I'm 23 and I was born on 23rd March 1986.

Reporter: _____ ?

Lady GaGa: I'm a singer, but I have also written songs for stars like Fergie, The Pussycat Dolls, Britney
Spears and others.

Reporter: _____ ?

Lady GaGa: My first album was called The Fame.

Reporter: _____ ?

Lady GaGa: My greatest hits are 'Just Dance' and 'Poker Face'.

Reporter: _____ ?

Lady GaGa: Yes, I learned to play the piano at the age of four.

Reporter: _____ ?

Lady GaGa: I was 13 when I wrote my first song.

Reporter: _____ ?

Lady GaGa: One of my best friends is Lady Starlight.

Reporter: Thanks for the interview. If your fans want to find out more about you,

_____ ?

Lady GaGa: They can go to my official website, www.ladyGaGa.com.

Reporter: Great. Thank you and bye.

Lady GaGa: Bye.

b) *Now use the information from the interview to write a short biography of Lady GaGa. If you need more
information you can do some research on the internet. Don't forget to check your text when you have
finished!*

A postcard

a) *Read the postcard.*

Dear Mr Schmidt,

Hello from Birmingham. We are here for the Music for Youth Festival. The people here are really nice and friendly. The music teachers are great, but the hostel is a bit old and the rooms are small. Yesterday I played the drums with five others. In the evening I went to a café with some friends. Birmingham is an interesting town. The weather is OK, but we're inside all day. Tomorrow is our big day – it's our concert!

See you next week in class!

Yours,

Markus Stein

Oliver Schmidt

Lindenstr. 12
14057 Berlin
GERMANY

b) *Use the words in the lists to write your own postcard in English to a teacher at your school. Use one word from each group.*

Places	People	Hotel	Yesterday	Weather	Tomorrow
England	friendly	super	swimming	terrible	museum
The Harz	fun	cold	shopping	rainy	disco
Italy	loud	old	surfing	hot	disco
Berlin	boring	big	restaurant	windy	sights

Hannah's e-mail

Read Hannah's e-mail to her friend Jody. Answer Hannah's e-mail for Jody. Use the words and phrases from the

1. no problem
2. crazy teachers too – read 2 books – but: history presentation very good
3. sorry – terrible – teacher – talk to him or her
4. fly – 1 August – three weeks – postcard: yes, if …
5. …

From:	Jody	⌄	🖾
To:	Hannah		
CC:			
Subject:			

Dear Jody,
I am sorry that you had to wait so long for my answer.

Dear Hannah, _____

I have been very busy with lots of work for school. Sometimes our teachers have crazy ideas. They want us to work so hard. How was your history presentation about children in Welsh coal mines?

_____

_____

_____

In the last few weeks I have had trouble with some of my classmates. They always take my school things away and hide them somewhere and I get into trouble if I can't find them in time for the lesson. Sometimes they call me names or make things difficult for me on the school bus. Tell me what you think about it. Should I tell my teachers? ☹

_____

_____

_____

Are you still planning to go to South Africa in the summer? I think that's such an exciting plan! I would love to go there. When are you going there? How long are you staying in Africa? Can you send me a postcard for my collection?

_____

_____

_____

Write soon – I need your help! Hannah.

_____

The music festival

Use the information to write a report about the music festival.
Try to use some linking words like after, *although, because, but, so, when.*

Weather – Friday: dry and sunny – Saturday: rain (not a lot) – Sunday: hot and sunny

last weekend – for three days – Friday 4 pm – Sunday 4 pm

buy food and drink – can sleep in stadium – bed & breakfast (cheap) – hotel (nice, expensive)

football stadium – near Bristol, England – easy to get to – train and bus

different live music – fun for everybody – rock, pop, heavy metal – dance all day

lots of groups, singers, bands – from England, Scotland, Wales – special guest: popstar from America (Rihanna)

The Music Festival

Foto: **Shutterstock.com** (dwphotos)

A weekend in autumn

Look at the story. Some parts are missing. Use your own ideas to complete the story.

One day two boys whose names were _____ and _____ wanted to

camp in the mountains. The weather was _____ so they packed some things in their

bags: a tent, _____ and _____. First, they took the bus to

_____.

From there, they walked into the forest to find a good place to camp.

They found a nice place. They had a beautiful view over the _____. So they put up their

tent, which was _____, and then they lit a fire. They had lots of things to eat with them

like _____ and _____.

When the fire was hot enough, they cooked _____.

Later they were tired and went to sleep. It was very quiet in the forest. They could only hear the

_____. Then one boy, _____, heard a noise. He looked out of the

tent and saw _____. He was very _____.

He called his friend, _____, and together they _____.

After that they _____.

In the end they made another fire and had a cup of tea and _____ for breakfast.

Illustration: **Roland Beier**, Berlin

A break in Central Park

Imagine you and your family spent a week in NYC.
One day you took a break in Central Park.

Look at the photo and write about your stay in Central Park.
Write about 100 words.

Think about – who was with you in the park
              – the weather on that day
              – what/who you saw
              – what you did
              – your feelings

Use adjectives, adverbs and linking words.

You can start like this:

After a lot of sightseeing, we wanted to relax a bit. So …

My stay in NYC

A one-week stay in New York City is over for you and your family. It's your last day. You're standing on an observation platform with your diary in your hands and have this view over the city.

Open your diary and write about the things you saw in NYC and how you felt there.

– What did you like best?
– What was interesting for you?
– What was not so good?
– Would you like to come again one day?

Write about 150 words.

You can start like this:

Dear diary

A wonderful week is over. How time flies.
We really had a nice stay. I …

OR

Dear diary

I'm so glad we're flying back
tomorrow. What an awful city …

Foto: **Shutterstock.com** (Songquan Deng)

A Thanksgiving party

Imagine you are staying with an American family for Thanksgiving. You have taken this photo and are mailing it to a friend in England.

Write an e-mail (about 100 words) about the Thanksgiving party.

Write – who was there
– what you did
– what you ate
– how you felt
– what you liked about the party
– why Americans celebrate it

A holiday in California

Your English teacher has asked the class to make a wall display on how you all spent your summer holidays. Imagine you spent your holiday in California.

Write a text of about 100 words for your display.

Think about – what is special about California / the people who live there
– what you can see and do there
– what you did (visit sights / national parks / fun parks)
– what you liked most / didn't like

You can start like this:

I was in California in my summer holidays. ...

One year at an American high school?

Would you like to move to America and go to an American high school for one year? Why or why not?

Write a text of about 150 words about what you think you would like or hate about moving to America (language, friends, family ...).

You can start like this:

I have often thought about applying for one year at ...

Foto: **Shutterstock.com** (Monkey Business Images)

Growing up in two cultures

Here is a comment on a Californian online forum for teenagers.

Read it and write an answer to it (about 80 words).

Say – who you are and where you live
  – what nationality you are
  – what language(s) you speak
  – what language(s) you are learning
  – what you think about Lian's life
  – why you agree or disagree with Lian

Lian H. (15) San Francisco, CA

I'm Chinese and I was born in California, so I'm a US citizen. My family is from Shanghai and when they first came to America, they only spoke a little English. Now my family speaks English, of course, but at home we speak Chinese. We eat Chinese food and do traditional Chinese things. So I still feel I'm growing up in two cultures. Where I live the different ethnic groups get on well together. I have never experienced any discrimination. There are lots of Chinese kids at my school and we learn about Chinese history and geography, but I don't like that – I want to learn about America and speak English. I think it is important that you learn the language of the country if you want to fit in.

An essay competition

You are spending a year abroad. At the Culture Club meeting you have been given the following flyer and have decided to take part in the competition.

Write your essay.

Hello! Hallo! Hola! Salut! Hej!

Can you say more than just hello in any language other than your own?
We think that foreign languages can open the door to the world!
Don't you agree?
But foreign languages are in danger in the United States of America!
Many American schools are giving up teaching foreign languages. Can you believe it?
We, The Institute of Foreign Language Teaching, are trying to fight back.
We are holding an essay writing competition.
Topic: Why foreign languages should be taught at all schools.
Tell us what you think. Share your experiences with foreign languages with us.
There are great prizes to win.
First prize: A four-week course in a foreign language of your choice.
Flights, four weeks in a hotel and all teaching materials are included.

Your essay should be about 200 words long.
Send it to The Institute of Foreign Language Teaching, Cleveland, OH, USA.

Schools around the world – MYM

Imagine you are on an exchange in Missouri and you have read Missouri Youth Magazine.

Write a letter to the magazine of about 150 words about German schools.

Tip: Brainstorm your ideas before you start writing.

Dear readers

Today we are starting a new series on schools around the world. If you have any experience of schools in other countries – write to us about it. We are interested in everything – school day, school year, vacations, subjects, etc. We are looking forward to hearing from you.

Yours
MYM

Girls' and Boys' Day

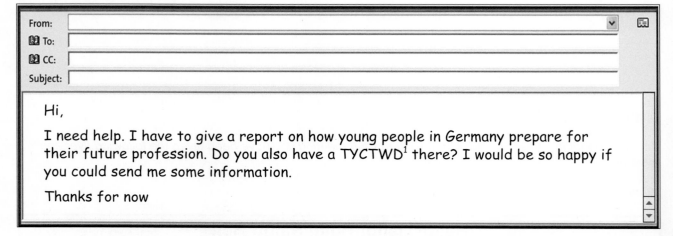

From:	
To:	
CC:	
Subject:	

Hi,

I need help. I have to give a report on how young people in Germany prepare for their future profession. Do you also have a TYCTWD[1] there? I would be so happy if you could send me some information.

Thanks for now

[1] *Take Your Child To Work Day*

To help your friend you have searched the internet and found the following information. Answer your friend's e-mail.

- 2001: Girls' Day started
- 2001: 1,800 girls took part
- 2010: 100.000 girls took part
- universities, research centres and companies are involved in the project
- for girls from class 5 to class 10
- girls and young women: think about school subjects and jobs which were traditional 'male subjects/jobs'
- girls and young women: get an idea of technical professions / see how exciting and interesting a career in industry can be
- not enough qualified junior staff in technical jobs
- some areas in Germany: also Boys' Day
- boys: get to know typical 'female jobs'

A report about an interesting event

Your school has got a partner school in the USA. Your class has started an internet blog to tell the American students about the highlights of your school year.

Today you have to write a report for the blog. You can write about a class trip / your project week or any other interesting event that has taken place at your school. Write 80–100 words.

Write about
- what/when/where/why
- what you liked about it
- what was special about it
- what you learned

Remember: Give your report a structure (beginning/middle/end).
Start a new paragraph for each new idea.
Start each paragraph with a topic sentence.

A postcard

You are on holiday and want to send a postcard to your American friend.

Write about 60 words.

Write about
- where you are staying
- who you are with
- your activities so far
- the weather

Start and finish your postcard in a friendly way.

Illustrationen: **Katharina Wieker**, Berlin

A help page

a) *This is part of an e-mail that Rabab, a 14-year-old girl from Pakistan, wrote to a teenage help page.*

Write a comment for the website. Give advice to help her. Write about 100 words.

> …
> I've lived in California now for five years, but I still feel lonely at school. The girls in my class always talk together in the break, but never to me. It's because I look different and I'm not interested in things they like – make-up or fashion.
> They hang out together after school. They go shopping, and do other stuff. They invite each other to their homes, but they never invite me. They do things that I am not allowed to do, like going to discos and parties. They talk about boys all the time of course, but I have never had a boyfriend. My parents want me to grow up in the culture of our home country. What can I do to find friends at school?
> Rabab K., L.A.

You can use these ideas or your own:

- invite the nicest girl to your home, she'll tell the others about you
- offer to help with homework in subjects that you're good at
- tell classmates about your home country and why your family came to the US
- join school clubs that bring you together with others, like a drama group or a dance class
- if things don't get better, talk to your favourite teacher about your problem

b) *Now you*

> Do you have classmates from other countries? If so, which countries are they from? Have you learnt about their cultures from them?

OR:

> Are you growing up in two cultures? Are you bilingual? Describe your class situation.

I am German but in my class there are lots of students who are not German. I think it is interesting to learn about different countries and cultures from classmates …

A letter to a magazine

a) *Complete the text.*

When you write to a magazine you can start your letter with _____ or 'Dear …' and the

name of the mag. People usually write to magazines to give their _____ about an article, or to

agree or disagree with someone's comment. But if you give your opinion, you should also give

_____ for your opinion. You can end your letter with 'Yours', 'Sincerely', or

_____.

b) *Write a letter to a magazine called 'Sixteen'. Write your opinion about German schools. What do you think is good and bad? For example, should the summer holidays be longer? What would you change if you could?*

You can start like this:

Dear Sixteen,

There are a few things about German schools that I would like to change if I could. For example, I don't like … There are some good things too. For example, …

A story

Here's the beginning of a story about Kerstin, a 14-year old German girl who is on a visit to her aunt and uncle in Atlanta.

Use your writing skills to write the middle and the end of the story. Give the story a title too. You can use the pictures for ideas or use your own imagination.

> It was Friday night. Kerstin had been in Atlanta for just one week, so everything was strange to her. The big house in Atlanta was still strange to her too. She didn't really like being alone at night in a strange house, but she wanted to do something for the family. The baby was sleeping, everything was quiet. Suddenly the phone rang. She jumped nervously. It stopped. Then it rang again. Should she answer it? She could only say that the family were out, but then the caller would know that anyway if she didn't answer the phone. It was still ringing. Then she thought she heard a knock at the window. Her heart started to beat loudly. Was there someone outside?
> …

Illustrationen: **Roland Beier**, Berlin

An article about the Grand Canyon

Last summer you visited the Grand Canyon with your family.

Write an article about this trip for the English language part of your school magazine.

a) *First look at the mind map and complete it with your own ideas and the ideas from the box.*

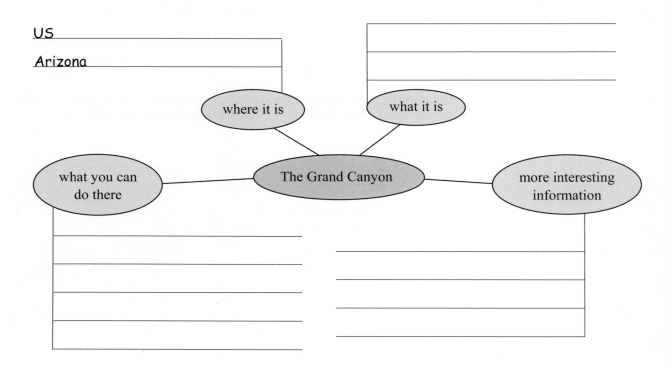

US

Arizona

where it is

what it is

what you can do there

The Grand Canyon

more interesting information

• deep gorge formed by Colorado River	• stay in the park overnight
• national park since 1919	• walk into the canyon on trails
• 5 million visitors every year	• walls of multi-coloured rocks
• mule trips	• Park Rangers look after park
• visit skywalk (good view)	• go rafting

b) *Then write a text of about 120–180 words.*

You can start your article like this:

The Grand Canyon
The Grand Canyon in Arizona is one of the most famous national parks in the US. The Canyon …

The travel blog

You've spent a weekend on Martha's Vineyard and have written down some notes about your stay.

Look at the map and notes and write an entry for your blog.

Write about 100–140 words.

How to get there
- by ferry (Vineyard Haven or Edgartown)
- by plane (Martha's Vineyard Airport)

Getting around
- by bus
- by car

Places to stay
- MV family campground
- seaside hotel at Oak Bluffs

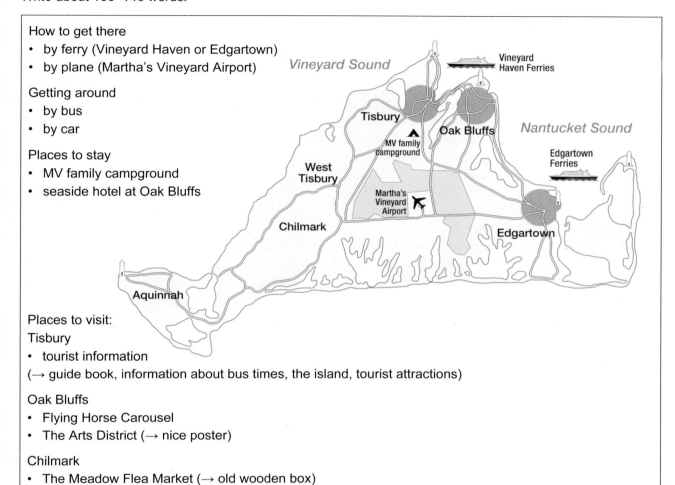

Places to visit:
Tisbury
- tourist information
(→ guide book, information about bus times, the island, tourist attractions)

Oak Bluffs
- Flying Horse Carousel
- The Arts District (→ nice poster)

Chilmark
- The Meadow Flea Market (→ old wooden box)

Wampanoag Tribal Center
- found out lots about the Wampanoag – First Thanksgiving!

Say something about …

- how you arrived at Martha's Vineyard.
- how you got from place to place.
- where you went shopping and what you bought.
- what you took photos of.

- where you spent the night.
- what the weather was like.
- what you liked doing and why.

You can begin your blog like this:

Hi folks. I'm back from Martha's Vineyard and …

Young firefighters California

Welcome to the young firefighters of California blog. This week it was ESD[1] California again and we would like to hear from you about it.

QUENCHO, 15 (San Francisco)

I've been a member of the young firefighters for eight months and I was very excited about ESD this year. At school I helped with a class of younger students and explained to them what they should do if an earthquake happens. Then we practiced in the classroom. I think they had fun AND learned some very important things. After school I went to the local shopping center where we gave out flyers. Next year I want to join the adult firefighters and train so that I can rescue people from buildings which have collapsed.

JACKERO, 17 (San Diego)

I've been reading all these blog entries and I want to say that ESD is absolute nonsense! I have had to survive so many ESDs and I still don't really know if I could do the right thing in an earthquake. Every year we do the same things, but if there really is an earthquake everything will be different anyway. And people will just panic no matter how many ESDs they have been through.

Add your own comment to the blog. Give your opinion on Quencho's or Jackero's comment and use what you know about fire practices at your own school to explain what you think. Write about 100 words.

[1] Emergency Services Day

A TV programme

You are planning a news programme for young people. Write about 100 words for a TV magazine.

Say – who the programme is for
 – what kind of news it will be about
 – who your reporters will be (young people?)
 – who will be in the studio (a live audience?)
 – what makes your news programme different from other news programmes

At the Maifest in Hermann

It all began at the Maifest in Hermann, Missouri last year. I was visiting my cousin Derek for the weekend. I had met him a few times at family parties, but I had never been to Hermann before. Before I went I spoke to Derek on the phone. 'Hey Jane,' he said, 'It's great that you can come and stay. It's the perfect time of year to visit Hermann, because the Maifest is on!' I wasn't sure what he meant so I asked him. 'OK, but what is the Maifest? I have never heard of it before.' Derek laughed. 'I can tell that you have never been to Hermann before. Everyone who knows Hermann knows the Maifest. It's a festival with traditional German dancing, bratwurst and beer.' 'German dancing? I'm not sure …,' I said. 'Don't worry,' Derek said, 'It's good fun for everyone!'

When I arrived in Hermann by bus, Derek was there to meet me. The journey had been very long, and I was a little bit tired. Derek was very excited and, while we were walking towards his parents' house, he talked nonstop. 'OK, the plan for tonight is to go to City Park for some fun rides with some friends of mine from high school. But before we go there we are meeting at Peter's house, he's probably my best friend, and after that …' I smiled as I tried to keep up with him and said, 'Derek – I only just arrived. Give me a break!'

Derek let me have a little break at home where his mom, my aunt Gracie, gave us some cookies and something to drink. At the kitchen table she explained about the old tradition of the Maifest. 'Hermann has been celebrating the Maifest since the early 1870s when the event was an end-of-school picnic. Children dressed up in their best Sunday clothes and marched behind the band, which played traditional German music. Later in City Park the children were given knackwurst and pink lemonade!' 'Oh please Mom, no history lesson now – we need to go.' 'OK, have fun tonight,' said Gracie as we left the house. The evening went on as Derek had said before. After we had met everybody at Peter's house, we went to City Park and had a good time there. The evening was great but what I will always remember is the moment when Peter's grandpa came along and said 'Guten Abend!' to us. At first I didn't understand but then I realized that he was speaking German. Later Peter explained that his ancestors had come to Hermann from Germany and that until World War I, German was the main language spoken in Hermann. 'We still speak German at home!' Peter explained. Then he smiled at me and I was a little bit embarrassed because this cute guy was looking right at me and I was sure I was going all red in the face. When we were walking to City Park, Peter was next to me and we started talking about our favorite music and our hobbies. Peter looked at me surprised when I told him that I loved cycling. 'One day I would like to take my bike to Europe and cross the Alps by bike,' I said. He smiled at me and I smiled back. 'You won't believe me when I tell you that I have a map of the Alps on the wall in my room!' he told me.

Peter and I have been chatting every day since that Maifest weekend, about bikes, tours and everything else and – well, maybe one day I will learn some German too.

Read the story and summarize it.

a) *What are the most important events of the story? Who did what when, where and why? Make some notes.*

b) *Use your notes and write a summary of about 10 sentences.*

You can start you summary like this:

The story is set in May last year. Jane goes to Hermann, …

A visit to New York City

Look at the photo of Times Square. Imagine you are one of the tourists there. Write about 150 words for a blog on your visit to New York City. The following questions can help you.

– Who was in Times Square with you?
  Who else was there? Why were you there?

– What did you see and do while you were there?
  What could you hear or see?
  What was the weather like?

– Where did you come from? Where did you go afterwards?

– When did you arrive? When did you leave?

– How did you like it there? How did you get there?
  How did you feel? How long did you stay?

About your favourite film

Your American friend is the editor of a school magazine. He has asked some students to write about their favourite films.

Write a short text of about 100 words about one of your favourite films.

Write about – the name of the film and what it is about,
  – when and where you saw it,
  – the characters in the film,
  – why you liked the film.

Foto: **Shutterstock**.com (Songquan Deng)

Indian proverbs

Look at the following Native American proverbs. Write a short essay on two of the proverbs. Say what you think about them, explain what you think they mean and why you like them. Write about 100 words on each. The phrases in the box can help you.

> I think … – The way I see it … – I still believe … – In my opinion … – In my view …

Take only memories, leave nothing but footprints.
(Chief Seattle)

Whatever happens to the earth happens to the children of the earth.
(Chief Seattle)

One finger cannot lift a small stone.
(Hopi)

Those who have one foot in the canoe, and one foot in another canoe, are going to fall into the river.
(Tuscarora)

I am a red man. If the Great Spirit had desired me to be a white man he would have made me so in the first place.
(Sitting Bull)

An article for a school magazine

Your school is participating in a project with a US High School in Kansas City. You and your American partner have worked on the topic 'Extracurricular activities in Germany and the USA – a comparison'. Your partner has asked you to write an article on this topic for the school magazine of his high school.

Write about 200 words.

- Write what you know about extracurricular activities in a US High School.
- Describe the extracurricular activities at your own school.
- Compare the two schools.
- Say what extracurricular activities you have done or still do.
- Say which American extracurricular activities you would be interested in and give reasons.

Illustrationen: **Henning Ziegler**, Berlin

Books or digital texts?

The governor of California wants to get rid of all textbooks in schools. The students should use computers and digital texts all the time.

In a forum on a website for teenagers you have found two comments. Write a comment too. Start with your internet name and where you come from. Explain which comment you are commenting on, what you agree or disagree with and why. Write about 150 words.

surferboy
mood: ☺ fine

Join Date: 8th June 2009
Location: Los Angeles
Posts: 328

Hey everyone! What a great idea to get rid of those old books. Some of them were probably used by my parents when they were at school. I use my computer all the time and get all my information from the internet. It would be great if we could do that in school too.

littlemissbookworm
mood: ☹ serious

Join Date: 21st August 2009
Location: San Francisco
Posts: 104

Hi surferboy! I don't think you are quite right. Books are useful too and not all of them are that old. I think that we should still have some good books and also learn how to use digital information properly.

A letter

You are spending a high school year in the USA and have become a member of the health club where you have been discussing healthy food at schools. Your high school sells fast food from a well-known fast-food chain and lots of other unhealthy food.

Write a formal letter to Mr Kendal, the principal of your high school in which you describe the differences between the two schools you know and explain your position.

First day back

Summarize the following story.

FIRST DAY BACK by Jonathan Gole

When the new school year started I couldn't quite believe that the holidays were already over. I had had such a great time with my cousin Dean. My parents took him and me to Alaska and we spent days exploring the wilderness. We saw dear and even a fox in the woods and we went swimming in the crystal clear water of some of the lakes. It was quite incredible to be the only ones who were swimming there at the time. The quietness and dark forest around!

And there I was back at school. Standing in front of my open locker I was wondering how I could cope with lessons again. Books and homework – not my kind of thing! I was still standing there unsure what to take out of the locker and what to leave in it when I realized that the locker next to mine had been taken over by a new girl. The year before that locker had belonged to a big guy called Gary who played football and lived on a farm on the road to Minneapolis. I glanced over at the girl and saw that she had brown hair and a nice and friendly face. As I was staring at her she looked over and we both said 'Hi!' at the same time. That made us both laugh.

Then the bell went and I walked quickly towards the science lab because Mr Brown didn't like anybody being late for his class. I was still thinking about that girl when Mr Brown had finished his second experiment.

At recess everybody was gathering round the bulletin boards in the hallway to sign up for the extracurricular activities. The new girl was standing there too, looking at all the different posters. Then she quickly wrote down her name, turned round and crashed into Mrs Pitts who was trying to find out if anybody had signed up for her Pottery Club. The new girl said sorry and left in a hurry. She must have been embarrassed. When Brian came up to me and said: 'Hi, Jonathan, are you up to a game of basketball after school?' I wasn't paying attention. I was only trying to read the names on the lists to find an unfamiliar one. 'Hi, Brian, yeah, sure!' I said absentmindedly. Brian smiled and said: 'Great! I went to a basketball camp with the Missouri Tigers this summer!'. Sarah Willis, Jane Ogden, Prisca Plotka, there it was: Jenny Wilkins. The only name on the lists I didn't know and I was going to put my name underneath hers! But then I realized that she had written her name on the list for the Poetry Club! The Poetry Club! I just couldn't believe it. Why did this have to happen to me? I was the last person in the entire universe who would have signed up for a club like this. I was useless at English!

I breathed hard and continued to read: 'First meeting on Friday after school. Everybody must write a poem about nature and bring it to the meeting so we have got something to discuss.' My head went slightly dizzy. About nature? When I closed my eyes I could still see the beautiful scenery in Alaska. Perhaps? I wasn't sure. But that would be a good chance to meet Jenny Wilkins.

Take your dog to work day

Last Thursday was 'Take your dog to work day'. Many people took their dogs to work and lots of surprising things happened.

Choose one situation and write a story. Remember to

- brainstorm your ideas.
- organize your ideas.
- outline your story (beginning, middle and end)
- choose a narrator (The person who took their dog to work or somebody who met owner and dog.)
- make the beginning of the story interesting.
- use adjectives, relative clauses, linking words, time phrases, …
- check your story for mistakes.

Laura Bowler, who works as a taxi driver, took her dog to work.

James Knight took his dog to the shoe shop where he works as a shop assistant.

Bob Miller teaches at a primary school and took his dog to work there.

Illustrationen: **Henning Ziegler**, Berlin

Writing a formal letter

a) *Complete the text with words and phrases that are correct for formal letters.*

You put your own address _____, but you don't write your name. Under your address you

write _____. The address of the person you are writing to is written _____.

You begin a formal letter with '_____' when you don't know the name of the person

you are writing to. Remember that the first word of the first paragraph starts with a _____

letter – which is different from German. You shouldn't use _____ forms in formal

letters. Write 'I am' and 'I would' instead of 'I'm' and 'I'd'. You finish a formal letter with

'_____' if you don't know the name of the person you are writing to. If you know the

name, you start with '_____' and you finish with '_____'.

b) *Lina Schneider from Munich writes a letter of application for a job as assistant receptionist at a hotel in London for six weeks in the summer. What belongs where in a formal letter? Choose the correct parts from the list on the right and write the number in the correct place in the letter below.*

(letter layout with blank boxes)	1 Best wishes
	2 Yours faithfully
	3 Dear Mrs Wilson
	4 2nd May 2014
	5 Dear Sir or Madam
	6 I look forward to hearing from you.
	7 I am writing to apply for the job of assistant receptionist as advertised on your website …
	8 Webergasse 8 81235 Munich
	9 The Manager Lancaster Hall Hotel 28 Lancaster Road London W8 IJL

Lina Schneider
Lina Schneider

c) *If you wanted this job, how would you write your letter of application? Write the main text of your letter. Include the following:*

– your personal details
– how long you have been learning English and how good your English is
– what kind of person you are, work experience, your hobbies and interests
– why you would like the job and why you think you could do it well.

Writing a CV

Lina has to enclose her CV with the application. Here is the necessary information about her:

> Her telephone number is 0049 89 612 3797. Her mobile number is 0173 835 2380.
> Her e-mail is: lschneider@afl.com
> She was born in Munich on 23rd November 1998.
> Lina is a friendly, hard-working student who likes speaking English and enjoys meeting people. She is good at organizing and likes working in a team. She is punctual and reliable.
> She has already worked as a waitress for six weeks in a hotel in Stockholm, Sweden, where she spoke English and German to hotel guests. Last year in the Easter holidays she also worked at the information desk in a shopping mall in Munich for two weeks.
> In her free time she likes reading and writing to online friends in the UK and the USA. She enjoys cooking, swimming and playing tennis. She is a member of the school drama club.
> Lina was at primary school in Augsburg from 2005 to 2009. She has been at secondary school in Munich since 2009. She is taking her school-leaving exams (similar to A-Levels) this year. She has a good level of everyday English (six years) and French (four years). She also has good computer skills and a moped licence.

a) *In what order should Lina present this information at the top of her CV? Write numbers 1–6.*

☐ Postal address   ☐ Mobile number   ☐ Name
☐ E-mail address   ☐ Date of birth   ☐ Place of birth

b) *What could Lina write in her short personal statement?*

_____

_____

c) *In which order should she give details about the following? Write 1–6.*

☐ Work experience   ☐ Hobbies and interests   ☐ Education
☐ Qualifications   ☐ Reference(s)   ☐ Other skills

d) *Now use information in* **a)** *to write the CV sections in* **c)***, but leave out 'Reference(s)'. Remember to write notes, not full sentences.*

_____

_____

_____

_____

_____

_____

_____

_____

e) *Write the CV using the correct format.*

_____

Applying for a job

Sue Evans lives in Bristol. She has seen the advert below and wants to apply for the job.

Write her application letter. Write something about her skills and why she would be the right person for this job.

The Bristol Times   2 November 2013

St. John's Residential Care Home

At St. John's we have 80 residents and consider it extremely important to offer each one of them a wide range of free-time activities.

We are looking for a **young volunteer** (m/f) to teach a small group (12 people) basic computer skills, including using the internet and writing e-mails. The classes would take place once a week for one hour. If you know how to use the internet effectively and know a bit about downloading programs and how to surf the internet safely, you are the right person for this job! And don't be afraid – you don't have to be an internet expert to apply, but you should be able to explain things so that your 'students' find their way round the internet.

Are you interested in working with people and sharing your IT skills?

We would provide training after Christmas. Please tell us which days of the week would suit you best.

Sorry, we can't pay anything, but we will be happy to give you a reference.

Please send your application letter plus CV to:

Ms Alice Spring
St. John's Residential Care Home
4 New Garden Street, Bristol BS1 3AD

Foto: **Shutterstock.com** (Paul Vasarhelyi)

A summer course in Britain

You have found this advertisement for a summer course and want to apply for a grant[1].

Write your letter of application and your CV including a personal statement.

Summer course in Britain?

Our English junior summer courses take place at Sunshine College in Brighton during the months of July and August.
We offer pupils ages 13–18 years the opportunity to combine learning English with sports, activities and visits to places nearby.
Each year we offer grants[1] to five German pupils.

Send us you application to be one of them.
Send your application to:

Sunshine College
100 Church Street
Brighton
East Sussex
BN2 1 UD

---

[1] grant *Stipendium*

A year abroad

Imagine you have spent a year at an American high school as an exchange student. At the end of the year the organization asks you to write an article about your stay there, which will be published in an international youth magazine.

Write the article and comment on your experience. Describe your school, your daily routine and discuss advantages and disadvantages of such a school year abroad. Write at least 200 words.

- Highline High School in Burien, near Seattle
- 1500 students; school starts at 8 am and finishes at 3 pm
- extracurricular activities: volleyball, soccer, cross-country racing, basketball, drama, big band
- host family: Mike and Judy Todd, two sons who do not live at home any more, the cat Felix
- their jobs: Judy – sports teacher at Highline High School, we went to school together by car, Mike – volleyball coach
- her free time: walking, gardening, badminton, cinema
- his free time: table tennis, volleyball, cinema

Here are some more ideas to help you:

> my first week there – how I made friends – high school dances – free time – nice house and/but ... –
> helping at home – speaking English all day – farewell party ...

Me Down Under!

You're spending your summer holidays travelling in Australia. You've promised to let your friends know what you're doing while you're 'Down Under'.

Write a blog about at least four days of your trip (the days don't necessarily have to be in the same week). Describe the following aspects of your journey:

– Where are you going and what have you already seen?
– Who's with you and how are you getting along? Have you met any new people?
– What do you find most impressive? What do you like? What don't you like?

Don't forget to describe your feelings – both positive and/or negative.

You can start like this:

> 21st July
>
> I have just landed in Sydney and I'm so tired. I couldn't really sleep on the plane because I was so excited. I'm writing from the hotel computer, ...

An e-mail from Hong Kong

You're Cath from Hong Kong and you're going to write your second e-mail to Jeannie in Queensland, Australia. This time you're going to include some facts on your city because Jeannie asked you to help her with a Geography presentation she wants to do on Hong Kong.

Write an e-mail to Jeannie and tell her about Hong Kong and your life in the big city. Ask her some questions too. The fact sheets below will help you. Write about 200 words.

Hong Kong

Hong Kong is part of China, but has its own government. British colony for 99 years, went back to China in 1997.

Population: 7 million

Ethnic groups: 95% Chinese, 2% Filipino, 3% other

Main religions: Buddhists/Taoists: 700,000

Christians: 560,000, Muslims: 90,000

Official languages: Chinese (Cantonese), English

Economy: important centre of trade and finance, tourism

Sights: Victoria Peak (mountain with great views of the city), Big Buddha (huge bronze Buddha statue on Lantau Island), harbour with impressive skyscraper skyline

Teenagers in Hong Kong

School: school uniform, teachers very strict, lots of homework, pupils need very good marks to get into university

Hobbies: movies, sport, karaoke, shopping, fashion (especially styles from Japan and Taiwan)

Good things: great for shopping, food from all over Asia, public transport (buses, trams, minibuses, ferries, subway, taxis)

Bad things: high levels of pollution

An e-mail to your best friend

You have a problem you need help with. You can't talk to your classmates or parents about it.

Write an e-mail to your best friend who has just moved to another town. You ask him or her for advice. Include the following points:

– describe your feelings
– give reasons for your feelings
– describe an event from last week

– say how you have tried to deal with your problem
– explain what your classmates/parents say/do
– ask your friend a question

Start like this:

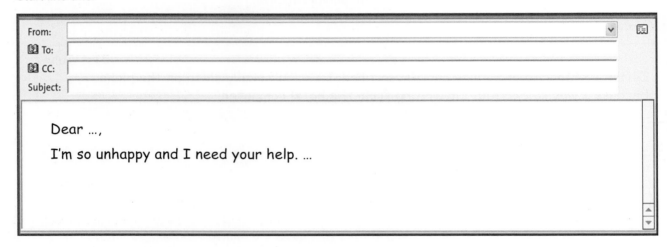

From:
To:
CC:
Subject:

Dear ...,

I'm so unhappy and I need your help. ...

Community service for everybody?

Everybody should have to do 12 months of community service after leaving school.

Write a text of at least 200 words on this topic. Your text should include the following points:

– arguments for and against
– examples to support your arguments
– your personal opinion

You can use the following ideas:

– different situation for boys and girls
– different kinds of community service
– the length of time
– the things you might learn
– …

Foto: **Shutterstock.com** (Lisa F. Young)

Making politics interesting for teenagers

Read the following flyer from the international organization 'Young Politics Worldwide', then write an e-mail of at least 200 words with your suggestions.

YPW Young Politics Day (March 1st)

Are you between 14 and 18 years old?

Do you think that politics are for old people?

Would you like to change that?

Then you are qualified to become one of our experts!

Help us to make politics more interesting for teenagers!

Tell us your ideas, e.g. on the following points:

- What's wrong with politics and politicians at the moment?
- Which political topics are teenagers especially interested in – and which ones aren't they interested in?
- Which media should be used to activate young people – and how?
- What kind of campaign events could be interesting for teenagers?
- What would your ideal politician be like?
- etc.

Write an e-mail to: info@ypw.org

Should the voting age for national elections be lowered?

In some German town and regional elections, 16-year-old teenagers are allowed to vote, but in national elections in Germany, just as in Britain or the USA, the voting age is still 18 years. Do you think younger teenagers should also be allowed to vote for the Bundestag, House of Commons or Congress?

a) *Make a list of the pros and cons of allowing younger teenagers to vote in the important national elections. You could consider aspects like:*

- life experience
- knowledge
- interests
- (in)dependence
- other responsibilities/duties/activities of 16-year-olds
- etc.

b) *Discuss the question in an essay of at least 200 words. Don't forget to write an introduction, a well-structured main part and a fitting conclusion.*

Feeling homesick

On the plane to Australia, Melanie met Aurélie, a girl from France. Aurélie is also an exchange student and is staying with a family on a farm near Melbourne. The two girls often write e-mails to each other. In her last e-mail Aurélie was feeling very homesick and lonely.

Write Melanie's reply (about 200 words).

You can include …

– Melanie's own experience on the cattle farm,
– her feelings,
– questions about Aurélie's life and feelings,
– some advice.

You can start like this:

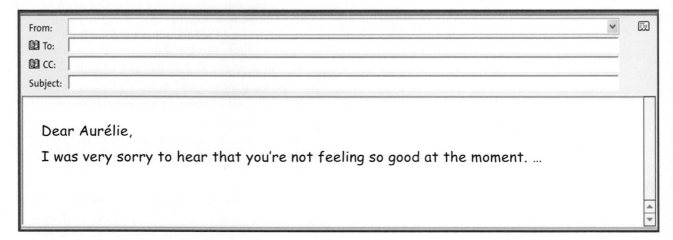

From:
To:
CC:
Subject:

Dear Aurélie,

I was very sorry to hear that you're not feeling so good at the moment. …

Social networking sites – an essay

You have been asked to write an essay for the school magazine about the pros and cons of Facebook and other social networkings sites. In your text explain what social networking sites are, what you see as their benefits and what the possible negative aspects for users are. Write about 120 words.

You can start like this:

Social networking sites are …

Australian Aborigines

A sad and often unknown part of Australia's history is the story of the Aborigines or Aboriginals. You have decided to write a report about the Australian Aborigines for your school magazine.

Use the fact sheet below to write your text.

PAST:
- 40,000 years ago developed oldest rock art in the world
- 19th century: Aborigines had to move because of European settlers; Aborigines who did not go were killed
- Europeans thought Aborigine culture was primitive
- Number of Aborigines reduced
- 1963: right to vote for Aborigines
- Until 1970s: Aboriginal children taken away from families

TODAY:
- Australia's population: more than 20 million, approx. 2 % Aborigines
- Some still don't live in the same place their whole lives, move around within a limited area, some live in tribes
- Oldest members make decisions
- Problems: discrimination, poverty, too much alcohol, unemployment

International work camps

What do you think about volunteering for work abroad? Think of arguments for and against working at an international work camp. List advantages and disadvantages. Write about 150 words. Remember to use paragraphs, topic sentences and your writing skills.

You can start like this:

Young people often decide to volunteer for work after school, before they start university or in the summer holidays ...

Foto: **Alamy**, Abingdon (Alan King engraving)

Landslide hits an orphanage

Read this article, taken from a newspaper. Then do tasks a) and b).

Landslide[1] hits orphanage[2] – six children dead

Six children lost their lives today when a landslide hit an orphanage in a peaceful village near Mumbai. 'I heard a loud noise and suddenly I was covered in earth and dust. I had to run for my life,' said eye-witness Terki Suleiman.

Hundreds of rescue workers tried their best to find survivors, but after five hours searching they had only found dead bodies.

'I was the one who found the first child,' said Andy McDowell, a volunteer with the Red Cross in India. 'I couldn't stop crying. I just can't believe what happened here.'

Not all the bodies have been found yet, but six children aged eight to ten are believed to have lost their lives in the landslide. The boy found by McDowell was taken to hospital immediately, but he could not be saved. 'It was too late for him,' Martin Andrews, a doctor at the Red Cross Hospital Mumbai, explained. 'When I examined him, I couldn't do anything more for him.' The landslide is a disaster for the orphanage, which is in a poor region of India. Three adults, who were working at the orphanage, are also reported missing.

Local charities and this newspaper had warned officials that the orphanage buildings were not safe and that there might be a catastrophe. But they were not listened to! Now it is the children who have to pay the price!

It was still raining when our reporter arrived at the scene. 'This terrible rain is preventing us from trying to rescue the missing boys and girls,' McDowell told us. More than 100 officials, firefighters and volunteers from the Red Cross stood in a circle unable to believe what had happened. 'The children were having their dinner when the mud fell over them,' said Geraldine Guetta, manager of the orphanage, wiping away her tears. 'The roof couldn't carry the heavy load and collapsed, burying the children underneath it. They didn't have time to escape.'

Nearby buildings have been evacuated as officials fear another landslide tonight.

[1] landslide *Erdrutsch* – [2] orphanage *Waisenhaus*

a) *Write a summary of the article.*

b) *Write a report for your school magazine about the accident. Inform your fellow students and give the most important facts.*

Discrimination?

a) *Read the article and label the elements 1–4.*

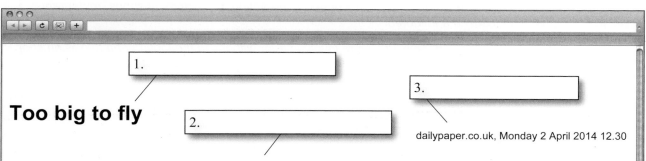

1. _____

Too big to fly

2. _____

3. _____

dailypaper.co.uk, Monday 2 April 2014 12.30

More and more airlines are thinking about introducing extra fares[1] for passengers who are obese[2].

One person, one seat, one fare – but what if one person can't fit into one seat? 'We used to give overweight passengers an extra seat whenever possible,' says Hugh Dickson, an *EnglandAir* spokesman. 'But given that the number of overweight passengers has risen significantly, the only way for us to guarantee them extra space is to either buy two economy seats or fly business class.' US airline *Americanwings* now wants to make people who are unable to squeeze into a single plane seat pay 75 per cent more. The decision was made for safety reasons: 'We have to make sure that the backrest can move freely up and down and that all passengers can use their seat belt'. They also argue it is costing them millions of dollars a year for the extra fuel.

Supporters are convinced by the airlines' arguments. 'If you went to a restaurant and ate two meals, you'd have to pay for two meals. Surely, if you go on a flight and take up two seats, you should pay for two seats,' says one angry passenger who felt very uncomfortable during a recent flight next to an overweight lady. 'We don't allow smokers to pollute our air so why should we allow fat people to occupy our seats?' Some people feel they are not being treated equally: 'I weigh 50 kilos and I'm only allowed 20 kilos for my bags. Why should someone who weighs 100 kilos be allowed 50 kilos extra?'

But opponents fear that if the new policy is adopted, it will have an impact on the right to equality. Most overweight people already feel discriminated against because people think they simply eat too much. But sometimes it is an illness along with physiological problems, so in some cases an obese person may actually count as disabled. 'The comments you hear are laughable,' says one such passenger. 'This is discrimination and hate speech. Flying is not very comfortable for us, either. I could just as well complain about people who smell, or screaming children on a plane. We are all human beings, no matter how much we weigh.' Another question is how to decide which passengers count as obese. Will passengers have to be weighed at the check-in counter? And what will happen when a passenger thinks he/she can fit into one seat, but the airline says he/she needs two? Both *EnglandAir* and *Americanwings* did not give a definite answer to this.

by Sara Lockheed

4. _____

[1] fare *Fahr-/Flugpreis* – [2] obese *fettleibig*

b) *List at least three arguments for and against extra fares for obese people.*

c) *What do you personally think of the problem? Write a comment of about 150 words.*

The London Riots

Between 6 and 10 August 2011, there were bad riots in several London boroughs, following the shooting of a man by the police in Tottenham, North London. Throughout the rioting, thousands of shops, restaurants, pubs and clubs were vandalized and looted.

Read the following statements by people who were involved in or witnessed the looting of a television shop in Hackney, London. Then write an objective report, which includes the important facts and no opinions.

It was on Sunday afternoon. There were hundreds of young people on the streets enjoying themselves. I went out to see what they were doing, and then I joined in. They were taking things from the local television shop, so I also wanted to have my share! Suddenly there were police all over the place. Everybody ran away, and the police only managed to catch a few of us. I remember that outside the shop a man tried to stop us. The stupid idiot was shouting, so someone knocked him over. Well, it's his own damn fault, isn't it? He was standing in the way. I picked up his mobile that was lying next to him. The police were just too stupid to catch us. And now I've got this cool DVD player for free!

I was in one of the two riot police units that were called out to Hackney on the 7th at 5:05 pm. I was a bit scared, to be honest. When we arrived at the scene, there must have been several hundred people on the streets. Some cars were burning. About thirty people were taking this television shop apart, most of them 14 to 18-year-olds. I went in with six other policemen. We only had batons, but the crowd started to run away without trying to fight back. I suppose they were all too busy carrying away the electronic equipment. We managed to catch eight looters. One of them even tried to hold on to a flat-screen television while he was being forced into the police car. I hope they will all get tough sentences!

I was upstairs in my flat in Hackney when I heard the sound of breaking glass and screams. When I came downstairs, more than fifty rioting youths were vandalizing my shop and stealing all the expensive electronic equipment! I was too shocked to do anything. That was probably a good thing because I'm sure they would have killed me! When the police arrived, everyone started to run away. I still can't believe it! Someone said the riots were all about justice and standing up against an unfair class society, so why did they ruin a poor guy like me?

My name's John Cole from Hackney. It's a rough area, but I've never seen anything like that before! So many kids on the streets looking for trouble, breaking shop windows and vandalizing cars! I could see twenty, maybe thirty people looting old Shazad Ali's shop! It was terrifying! I felt I had to do something, so I tried to stop one of the looters who came running towards me. I can't remember what happened then. The next thing I knew was that I woke up here in hospital. The doctor says I have serious head injuries, but I will probably be back to normal soon. And that's not all: my money and mobile phone are gone!

Sarah's problem

Write a reply to this mail from the problem page of a UK teen magazine. What advice would you give Sarah? Write about 100 words.

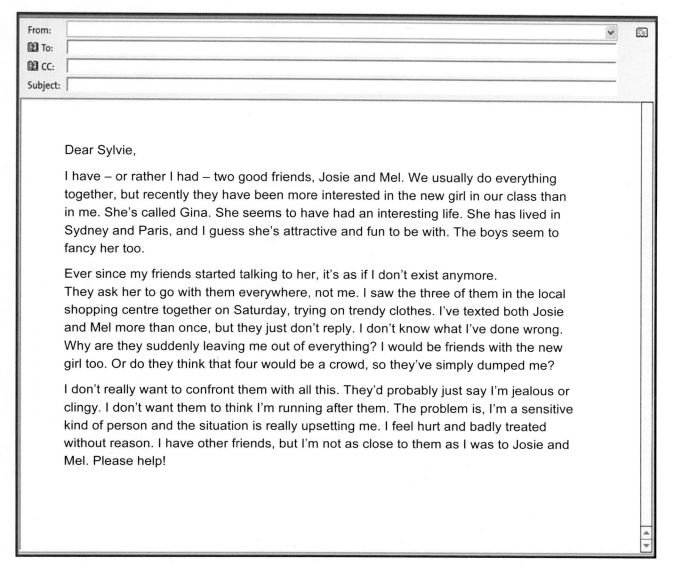

From:	
To:	
CC:	
Subject:	

Dear Sylvie,

I have – or rather I had – two good friends, Josie and Mel. We usually do everything together, but recently they have been more interested in the new girl in our class than in me. She's called Gina. She seems to have had an interesting life. She has lived in Sydney and Paris, and I guess she's attractive and fun to be with. The boys seem to fancy her too.

Ever since my friends started talking to her, it's as if I don't exist anymore.
They ask her to go with them everywhere, not me. I saw the three of them in the local shopping centre together on Saturday, trying on trendy clothes. I've texted both Josie and Mel more than once, but they just don't reply. I don't know what I've done wrong. Why are they suddenly leaving me out of everything? I would be friends with the new girl too. Or do they think that four would be a crowd, so they've simply dumped me?

I don't really want to confront them with all this. They'd probably just say I'm jealous or clingy. I don't want them to think I'm running after them. The problem is, I'm a sensitive kind of person and the situation is really upsetting me. I feel hurt and badly treated without reason. I have other friends, but I'm not as close to them as I was to Josie and Mel. Please help!

A report

Choose one of the following topics and write a report of about 150 words.

1 Our last family holiday
2 My favourite film
3 A good day in town with my friend(s)

A picture story

Tell the story shown in the pictures. You may use the key words or your own. Write at least 120 words.

Anna – boyfriend – dump

best friend – advice –
don't sit at home

decide – visit

leave home – moped – rain

on the way – stop – café – young guy

sit – next table – chat – laugh

leave café together – will meet again
next day – forget old boyfriend

What's your opinion?

Choose one of the following statements and write your opinion about it. Give reasons and examples where possible and sum up your opinion. Write about 150 words.

1 You can learn a lot about friends and relationships from TV and films.
2 Teenagers have problems, not just fun.
3 Teenagers spend too much time on computer and video games.

Illustrationen: **Constanze Schargan**, Berlin

A questionnaire

Answer the questions. Write about 120 words altogether.

---

* * *   QUESTIONNAIRE: FRIENDSHIP   * * *

1 How important is friendship to you? _____

2 What do you think is better and why: lots of friends or only a few really good friends?

3 How often do you see your best friend? _____

4 How much time do you spend with your friends every week? _____

5 How long have you known your best friend? _____

6 Which qualities do you look for in a friend? Explain why.

7 What hobbies or interests do you share with your friend(s)? _____

8 Nobody is perfect. What might cause you to break off a friendship? Give an example.

The right to strike

Read what a spokesman of the postal workers' union and some postal workers said at a strike meeting.
Mark the facts, not opinions. Then use the facts to write a short report.

The union has decided that postal workers will go on strike from Monday next week. There'll be a series of one-day strikes in different parts of the UK. The reason is that we think we are not being treated fairly by the management. There have been disagreements about pay, job cuts and changes to working conditions for a long time, but nothing happens. It's all just talk. Although there's less mail than there used to be, there's more work to do than ever before, but not more money. We're also afraid that our jobs are not safe.

Over 20,000 postal workers will be involved in England and Scotland, more than half of us in London, the rest in cities such as Bristol, Manchester, Edinburgh and Liverpool. Other cities will follow, I expect. We think it could be very serious because people are angry. A strike across Britain would involve about 160,000 workers. I imagine it would cost the country millions. And there will be public protests.

The action could lead to a nationwide postal strike in winter if the union doesn't come to an agreement with the management. But we have to strike. If workers up and down the country don't take a stand, the employers will never improve things for us. One thing is clear, this strike action will be the most serious for over three years.

You can start like this:

From Monday next week postal workers in the UK will go on strike. There will be a series of one-day strikes ...

Describing an object

Describe an electrical appliance in a short paragraph. You could choose something in the classroom, school, at home (kitchen, bathroom, garden) or something from your personal things. Use a dictionary for unknown words and spellings.

→Describe the object's **shape**:
  square, round, oblong, flat, narrow, wide, straight sides, long, short ...

→its **material**:
  made of metal, steel, wood, glass, plastic, paper, leather, even/uneven surface, waterproof, strong, heavy, ...

→its **size**:
  large, small, tiny, thick, thin, about ten centimetres, high, tall, wide, deep ...

→its **colour**:
  bright red, dark blue, -ish (yellowish) ...

→its **texture**: hard, soft, rough, smooth, sharp:

→its **general appearance**:
  looks like ... / is similar to ...

Start your description with the general appearance. Then continue with details, like colour, etc. Use comparisons, for example for the size (bigger than ..., not as big as ..., about the same size as ...). Be as exact as possible. Use suitable adjectives, relative clauses, linking words, passive verb forms. Write in the present tense.

My object is ... / The object I am describing is ...
I'm going to describe something that ...

Foto: **Shutterstock.com** (1: vetkit, 2: ndphoto, 3: Singkham, 4: imagedb.com)

Making school greener

Think of arguments for and against the statement below and present them in an argumentative text.

> **We can do more to make a school greener.**

1 Brainstorm your ideas and write notes.
2 Order your ideas for and against the statement.
3 Think of reasons or examples to support your arguments.
4 Write an outline:

1 **Introduction** (your topic and why it is important)
 This topic is very important because …

2 **Arguments** (write arguments **for** and **against** the statement)
 On the one hand, … A lot of people think that … First, … A good example of this is …
 Another reason is that … Second, … Finally, … However/Fortunately/Sadly, … On the other
 hand, … Another argument is that …

3 **Conclusion** (sum up the arguments and give your own point of view)
 In my opinion, it is clear that … To sum up, I think … That's why …

Remember that it is often better to begin with the point of view that you don't support. If you think students and teachers can make school greener, first say why some people think they can't do so.

> **INFO BOX**
> More than 12 000 UK schools (over 50%) have joined the Eco-Schools international
> environmental programme. According to this programme, the following sums of money are
> spent in UK schools every year: over £200 million on electricity and water, over £150
> million on paper and writing materials and more than £56 million for rubbish collection.
> Member schools can win awards for 'green activities'. The highest is the Green Flag
> Award. Look up the website and see what you have to do: www.eco-schools-org.uk

The greenhouse effect

a) *Draw and label a diagram which shows the greenhouse effect. Use the internet and a dictionary.*

b) *Explain the greenhouse effect in about eight to ten sentences. The words in the box will help you. Use present tense active and passive verb forms.*

> absorb – atmosphere – burn – carbon dioxide (CO_2) – emit – emissions – energy –
> fossil fuels – greenhouse gases – heat – natural gas – oil – produce – reflect back – release –
> rise – space – store – sun's rays – temperature – trap

About job interviews

a) *Read the ideas below and add to them if you want. Then edit, order and number the list. Write your finished list.*

NOTES: JOB INTERVIEWS

- arrive ten minutes early
- dress neatly
- girls: not too much make-up
- boys: make sure your clothes are neat and tidy
- find out info about the company
- before the interview ask questions about the company
- keep eye contact with interviewer
- prepare to talk about your qualifications, skills and personal qualities

- speak clearly, not fast
- wait until you are offered a seat
- be polite and friendly
- show interest
- know your strengths and weaknesses
- talk about work experience
- don't ask about money
- send a short letter of thanks the next day
- say why you would be good for the job

---

b) *Use your ideas from* **a)** *to write a short article for your school magazine: 'What to do and what not to do at an interview'.*

Josie's trip

Improve the following sentences by adding suitable words and phrases. Use the words/phrases in the box or your own words. Read the text carefully first.

---

funny – brown – good-looking – interesting – old – small – sporty – terrible – unfaithful –
blond hair – excitedly – loudly – luckily – quickly – straightaway – **suddenly** – **one evening** –
the next day – in a few minutes – in the next town – on the way – all the time

---

One evening Josie **suddenly** received a text from her boyfriend, Tom. _____ she read his message, but she couldn't believe what it said – he had dumped her for another girl! Josie called her best friend _____ for advice. Her friend told her to keep busy and not to sit at home thinking about him _____. _____, Josie _____ packed her rucksack and left home on her _____ moped. The weather was just the way she felt – _____. It was raining. _____ she stopped at a _____ café _____. She didn't notice that a _____ young guy with _____ had also entered the café. He sat down at the next table. He was wearing a _____ jacket and jeans. He started an _____ conversation about mopeds and told a _____ story about his moped that made Josie laugh. They chatted and laughed a lot. Josie and the young guy left the café together, talking _____. _____, it had stopped raining. They planned to meet again the next day. And Tom? Who was Tom? Had she forgotten her _____ boyfriend already?

Mixed relationships

a) *Complete the sentences with a suitable linking word from the box.*

after – although – because – before – if – so – so … that – unless – **when**

1 **When** Dominic and Afra marry next week, it will be a Muslim wedding.

2 _____ there are some disadvantages to mixed relationships, there are also advantages.

3 _____ the partners are prepared to be tolerant there may be difficulties in the relationship.

4 Problems in mixed relationships often start _____ the couple have lived together for some time.

5 Sometimes the partners don't know much about each other's religion, _____ they are not tolerant enough.

6 Sometimes one partner changes to the religion of the other, _____ religious differences can be avoided.

b) *Connect the two sentences using the linking word in brackets.*

1 Mixed relationships were not easily accepted 50 years ago. They are more common nowadays. (which)

_____

2 Tina and Ranjiv have been together for two years. Ranjiv is a Hindu. (who)

_____

3 It is possible to live happily with a partner with a different religion. Successful mixed relationships prove it. (that)

_____

4 Not only religion, but also traditional beliefs play an important role. They are often very different. (which)

_____

c) *Rewrite the sentences without changing the meaning.*

Use: although – but   so – because   unless – if … not

Sometimes you have to change the sentence structure.

1 Often the partners in a mixed relationship may be happy, but their parents are not.

_____

2 If a partner's religious practices are not accepted by the other partner, a mixed relationship can fail.

_____

3 A relationship may fail because different religious practices can make everyday life difficult.

_____

4 The partners may want to stay together, but in everyday life love is sometimes not enough.

_____

© 2014 Cornelsen Schulverlage GmbH, Berlin. Alle Rechte vorbehalten.

Buying clothes from developing countries?

a) *Read the four parts of the text:*

Teenagers should not buy cheap clothes from developing countries.

☐ **Topic sentence:** _____

If we cannot be sure of the working conditions in the factories where they were made, we cannot be sure that child labour was not used. That is why consumers should be critical.

To sum up, I would like to say that fashion is quite important for young people, including me and my friends, but I think it is more important to be sure that children's rights are not being abused. That's why we should only buy clothes from countries that do not use child labour.

☐ **Topic sentence:** _____

Firstly, most teenagers are interested in fashion and trendy clothes but they do not have much money to spend. As a consequence they are happy that they can buy clothes cheaply, no matter where they come from. Secondly, you cannot always know the background of the clothes you buy. For example, they may have been made by adult workers for fair pay. Additionally, one can argue that buying clothes from developing countries helps poor people to earn some money. Even though working conditions are mostly bad, the hours long and the pay poor, it is better than having no work at all.

☐ **Topic sentence:** _____

It is important for teenagers to think about where the trendy fashions were made. Some people have a problem with buying clothes produced in poor developing countries because of the bad conditions for the workers there. Here in Europe these clothes are much cheaper than clothing designed and manufactured by European companies. So the question is: should we as teenagers support this trade and buy clothing from these countries or not?

☐ **Topic sentence:** _____

For example, if the label has no reliable information about the materials used, or if the country of origin is not given, consumers should be critical about buying. Secondly, conditions in clothes factories can be terrible. For example, there are some shocking reports about the working conditions and treatment of children being forced to work in small, dark rooms in clothes factories. Moreover, most of the money you pay for the goods goes to the clothing companies, not to the workers.

b) *Put the text parts in the correct order. Write the numbers 1–4 in the boxes.*

c) *Label the text parts in* **a)***:* Introduction – First point of vue – Second point of vue – Conclusion

d) *Choose the correct topic sentence for each text part and write A–D above the text.*

A̅ After looking at arguments for both sides, I think it is better not to buy clothes from developing countries.

B̅ Teenagers represent an increasing percentage of consumers buying clothes.

C̅ Lots of young people believe that buying clothes from developing countries is acceptable.

D̅ However, many people think there are more arguments against buying clothes from developing countries.

What's your opinion?

a) *Collect arguments for and against this statement:*

| A gap year brings more advantages than disadvantages. |

Notes: Advantages of a gap year after school

_____

_____

_____

_____

_____

Notes: Disadvantages of a gap year after school

_____

_____

_____

_____

_____

b) *Match the phrases below to the sections of the outline where you could use them (sometimes in two sections). Write the number of the section (1–4) next to each phrase.*

1 **Introduction** – the topic and why it is important

2 **Arguments** – first point of view

3 **Arguments** – second point of view

4 **Conclusion** – sum up the arguments and give your own point of view

In my opinion, it is clear that … ☐

On the one hand, … ☐

A lot of students think that … ☐

This topic is important because … ☐

A good example of this is … ☐

To sum up, I believe that … ☐

On the other hand, … ☐

It can also be argued that … ☐

One reason is that, … ☐

For example, I know … ☐

That is why I think … ☐

First/Second/Finally, Additionally, … ☐

Other people/students disagree. They think that … ☐

However, lots of people feel that … ☐

After looking at both sides, … ☐

So the question is, should … or not? ☐

c) *Use the information in **a)** and **b)** to write a discussion. Write 120–150 words.*

Writing a report

Whatever the subject, a good text gives the reader important information in the first few sentences: who the text is about, what happened or took place, where, when and why it happened and sometimes how it happened. The order is not always the same. Reports inform the reader about facts, not opinions.

a) *Read the following text and underline the information which answers the 5 Ws and How. Then make notes.*

On 8th December 1980 at 10.50 pm the former Beatle John Lennon was murdered by Mark David Chapman. Lennon was shot in the back four times with a revolver. The killing took place in NYC, at the entrance to the exclusive apartment house, the Dakota Building, on West 72nd Street, where Lennon and Yoko Ono lived. At the time of the killing the motive was unclear, but Chapman had a history of mental illness.

_____
_____
_____
_____
_____
_____
_____
_____

b) *Read the notes about an accident. Then use them to write a report for a local newspaper. Include all the facts and decide on a suitable order. Add some details to make your report realistic. Do not add any opinions.*

NOTES
boy, 13, doing newspaper round before school, bike, yesterday at 7.20 am, hit by a silver Toyota Auris, Willow Road Merton, car driving too fast, couldn't stop, roads wet, boy crossed road without looking, driver upset, boy taken St. Mary's hospital, treated for broken leg, shock

ACCIDENT REPORT

_____
_____
_____
_____
_____
_____
_____
_____
_____

c) *Write a short report about:*

A cultural event or a sporting event that I enjoyed

Making changes

Use your own words and shorten the sentences.

1 'It tells the story of Lindsey, a schoolgirl athlete who is training hard to be chosen for the British diving team at the London 2012 Olympics.' (26 words)

_____

_____

2 'Lindsey is upset about the break-up of her parents and rebels by missing her diving training to hang out one night in the park with a group of laughing, smoking, beer-drinking classmates, something she has never done before.' (38 words)

_____

_____

3 'Lindsey must decide whether to follow her Olympic dream or accept motherhood. She chooses to have the baby.' (18 words)

_____

_____

4 'Lindsey's sporting ambition is still alive, and she takes up her diving training again, supported by Robert.' (17 words)

_____

_____

A film review

Once a year your school publishes a newspaper edition in English. This time it is your turn to write a film review.

Choose a film you have seen recently and write a film review for the readers of the school newspaper.

Make sure your review

– has a title,
– gives basic information on the film (director, actors, country, genre, film start),
– describes the plot, the setting, the soundtrack and the film's message,
– gives us your point of view on the story, acting and characters, maybe special effects and camera work:
  • What is the overall effect?
  • How is the message conveyed to the audience?
  • What are the strengths and weaknesses of the film?
  • Would you recommend it?

If you are not sure about some details, you can just make them up. Write about 250 words.

Janka's e-mail

Correct this e-mail from Janka to her cousin in the UK. Mark the mistakes and correct them.

From:	
To:	
CC:	
Subject:	

Hi Becca!

Here I am at last! Sorry I didn't write to you since Christmas. I've been at home with a very bad cold since a week. I had a temperature too, so the doctor said I must to stay in the bed, but tomorrow I go to school again. My most interesting news are that I will do volunteer work after school, maybe in India for six months. My teacher gave me some advices, and I have got a lot of informations from the internet. Our neighbours daughter also has gone to India last year, and she has done some really intresting work in a school. I would like working on an environmental project. Mum has told to me that you have done volunteer work after you left school. What did you? Maybe we can talk over it when we come to Cambridge to Easter. I already look forward to see you all again. I'm sure we have a great time. I hope the whether will be good. If not, we can go shoping. And I'd like to go to London again with the train, and make some photos like we did last time.

OK. That's enough for today. I call you again soon, maybe next weekend.

Love to everybody,

Janka

Violation of human rights – here and over there

When we talk about violations of human rights, we mostly think of dictatorships or developing countries. Does that mean that there is no violation of people's rights in our society?

a) *Describe situations for which this is not true. Think of minorities, children's and women's rights, bullying at school or at work. Write about 150 words.*

b) *Is there a difference between human rights violations here and in other countries? What are we allowed to do if we feel that our rights are not respected? Describe different methods that people in Germany could use against violations of human rights. Discuss which ones you find most effective. Write about 150 words.*

Who needs parents?

The following statement was posted on the internet by a 16-year-old teenager:

Think about why you agree or disagree with this statement.

Write a text with an introduction and arguments for and against this statement. Don't forget to include a conclusion with your opinion at the end. Write about 250 words.

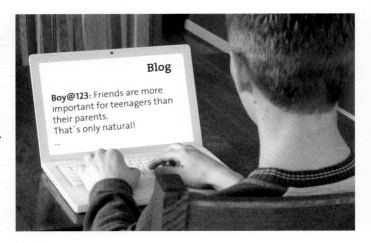

A letter to a friend

You have been an exchange student in England for four months. You think that Paul, your new friend at school, has got financial problems.

You don't want to talk to him directly, so you decide to write him a letter or an e-mail. You can use some of the following points, but you can also come up with your own ideas. Suggest things he could do to get out of this situation. Write about 250 words.

Dir ist aufgefallen, dass er nicht mehr dabei ist, wenn alle gemeinsam ausgehen. Vorher bist du bereits auf seinen Umgang mit Geld aufmerksam geworden. Er scheint viel für eines oder mehrere der folgenden Dinge auszugeben:
– Er hat jede Woche einen anderen Handy-Klingelton.
– Er verschickt ständig SMS und telefoniert lange mit seinem Handy – auch von zu Hause aus.
– Er hat oft neue Kleider und Schuhe, trägt sie aber nicht oft. Es sind meistens teure Sachen.
– Er bringt nicht wie andere Essen von zu Hause mit, sondern geht ständig in Fast-Food-Restaurants.
– Er kauft jede Woche Zeitschriften (Fußball-, Computer-, Jugendzeitschriften, etc.)
– Wenn ein neues Computerspiel herauskommt, hat er es oft sehr schnell.
– Er leiht sich immer wieder Geld und manchmal bekommt man kleinere Beträge nicht zurück.

A time capsule

Imagine it is the year 2050. In your town the foundation stone for a new solar plant is going to be laid. As usual, the foundation stone will contain a time capsule with relevant information on the time you are living in. Your school has been chosen to write texts that might be interesting for future generations – people who will find them in 100 or 200 years.

> ### What is life like in the year 2050?

Describe a typical day in the year 2050. Include information on where you live, how you get to school, what kind of energy you use, what you eat and drink, what you do in your free time, what your home looks like, how you travel etc. Write about 250 words.

Illustrationen: **Katharina Wieker**, Berlin

Cornelsen

Dream Deferred

Interpret this poem with the help of the tasks below:

Dream Deferred
by Langston Hughes

What happens to a dream deferred[1]?
Does it dry up
Like a raisin[2] in the sun?
Or fester[3] like a sore
5 And then run?
Does it stink like rotten[4] meat?
Or crust[5] and sugar over
like a syrupy sweet?
Maybe it just sags[6]
10 like a heavy load.
Or does it explode?

a) *State in your own words what happens according to the poem if a dream is deferred.*

Explain in your own words at least three of the six images in the poem. Refer to real-life situations or give other examples.

b) *Analyse how Langston Hughes uses the rhyme scheme and other poetic devices to underline the message of the poem. Don't forget to quote from the text and indicate lines.*

c) *Choose one of the following tasks (1 or 2):*

1 *Write one more verse for the poem with the help of the following pattern. You do not have to (but may of course) find rhymes:*

Does it _____

Like a _____

Or does it _____

Like a _____ ?

2 *Illustrate an example of a dream that should not be deferred in your opinion and explain why.*

[1] (to) defer (to) *delay* – [2] raisin *Rosine* – [3] (to) fester *eitern* – [4] rotten *verdorben* – [5] (to) crust *verkrusten* – [6] (to) sag *(to) hang down*

Text: **Langston Hughes**: Dream Deferred; Illustration: **Katharina Wieker**, Berlin

A poem

Write a poem on one of the following topics:

– parents and children
– a city/cities
– a nightmare
– the sky

Use the following steps to create your poem:

1 Choose your topic.
2 Decide what type of poem you want to write: a cinquain, a haiku, an acrostic, or a rhymed poem of 4–8 lines.
3 Brainstorm ideas for your poem in a mind map.
4 Write your poem. Try to use poetic devices (imagery, sound devices).
5 Find an interesting title for your poem.

Comment on your own poem

Explain the content and the form of your poem in full sentences.

– State why you have chosen your topic.
– Sum up in one or two sentences what your poem is about.
– Explain the title of your poem and what you wanted to express about your topic.
– State the type of poem that you have chosen and explain why you think it is a suitable form for your topic.
– Analyse the poetic devices in your poem and explain why you have used them.
– Write a conclusion.
– Describe the difficulties you had writing the poem and say how you like it now.